American
AUTOMOBILE
TRADEMARKS
1900–1960

C. H. Wendel

Motorbooks International
Publishers & Wholesalers ®

First published in 1995 by Motorbooks International
Publishers & Wholesalers, PO Box 2, 729 Prospect
Avenue, Osceola, WI 54020 USA

Motorbooks International is a certified trademark,
registered with the United States Patent Office

The information in this book is true and complete to the
best of our knowledge. All recommendations are made
without any guarantee on the part of the author or
Publisher, who also disclaim any liability incurred in
connection with the use of this data or specific details

We recognize that some words, model names and
designations, for example, mentioned herein are the
property of the trademark holder. We use them for
identification purposes only. This is not an official
publication

Motorbooks International books are also available at
discounts in bulk quantity for industrial or sales-
promotional use. For details write to Special Sales
Manager at the Publisher's address

Library of Congress Cataloging-in-Publication Data

Wendel, C. H. (Charles H.)
  American automobile trademarks/by C. H. Wendel.
    p. cm.
  Includes index.
  ISBN 0-7603-0005-4 (pbk.)
  1. Automobiles—United States—Trademarks—
Directories. 2. Trucks—United
States—Trademarks—Directories. I. Title.
  TL154.W446   1995
  629.222'0275—dc20   95-14589

On the front cover: The Packard family coat of arms was
adopted as the company's emblem in 1928. It is
interesting to note that this emblem, like thousands of
others from different companies, was never registered
with the U.S. Patent Office.

On the back cover, clockwise from top right: Checker
Cab Manufacturing Corporation, 1928; Stutz Motor Car
Company, 1927; Aerocar Company, 1906; White Motor
Company, 1924; Willys-Overland Company, 1946; Buick
Motor Company, 1904; Marmon Motor Car Company,
1935; Reo Motor Car Company, 1925.

Printed and bound in the United States of America

Contents

Introduction

Although this book illustrates nearly 800 different trademarks from nearly 400 different car and truck builders, these totals represent only a small fraction of the total activity from before 1900 up to 1960. Automobile manufacturers in the United States totaled several thousand different companies. A very few were ultimately successful, some enjoyed temporary rewards, and the great majority saw their dreams turn into debts and heartaches. Of course, there were a few enterprising folks who capitalized on human greed, both theirs and that of others, to set up fraudulent stock schemes and other illegal activities.

This book is the result of researching the weekly *Patent Office Gazette* up to 1960. This makes some 3,000 separate issues that were searched, both through the indexes, and by a visual look at each page in the weekly trademark section. Now that the project is completed, the Author can look back at somewhere in the vicinity of 2,000 hours of research, compilation, and writing time. Many additional hours were spent in the darkroom, attempting to convert images that were sometimes very poor into something suitable for a book such as this.

One point stands out above all others in regard to this project; the vast majority of automobile and truck makers never bothered to register their trademarks, if in fact, they even used a trademark at all! We would estimate that less than 10 percent of the auto and truck builders afforded themselves this protection. Had even one-fourth of them done so, this book would have taken on epic proportions!

From a typographic viewpoint, a study of the trademarks is very interesting. Many of the early marks, say up to 1910, used fancy scripts, scrolls, and other devices. By 1920, most of these had given place to modern designs of the period, with sans serif lettering being the rage.

From a historical viewpoint, the trademarks provide interesting bits of information. When a certain trademark was initially used is more often than not a significant piece of the historical puzzle. Subtle changes in company names or changes of address also add to the historical value of the trademarks. In this connection, the Author emphasizes that this book and the trademarks herein are presented solely for their historical value, and are neither intended to add to nor subtract from any company or any product in any manner whatsoever.

This book is arranged alphabetically by the name of the applicant. In some instances, a personal name was used, instead of the company name. Although consideration was given to arranging this title by tradenames, this would have disrupted the complete chronology of a given company, so it was decided to retain the same general form as was used in the *Patent Office Gazette.*

Particularly for truck manufacturers, additional information outside of their trademarks has been virtually impossible to locate. For these, and for companies for which no information has been found, the Author solicits additional information from the reader. Likewise, where errors or omissions occur, kindly contact the Author, in care of the publisher, Motorbooks International.

Finally, if this book provides its readers with some leisure time enjoyment and occasional reference use, then the Author will feel well rewarded for his efforts.

C. H. Wendel
January 18, 1995

Alphabetical List of Manufacturers

Aerocar Company, Detroit, Michigan

The Aerocar mark was filed February 23, 1906, concurrently with the establishment of the company. During 1907 the name was changed to Aerocar Motor Company, and in 1908 the firm disappeared.

Ajax Motors Company, Racine, Wisconsin

All-American Truck Company, Chicago, Illinois

Filed in 1919, the All-American mark claimed first use on March 25, 1918. Outside of this mark, we have found few other details on the firm.

Left
Not to be confused with a company having the same name at Seattle, Washington, this Racine firm operated in the 1925-26 period. The Ajax was built in the former Mitchell factory acquired by Nash in 1924. This mark was first used April 15, 1925.

5

**All-Car Unit Company,
Philadelphia, Pennsylvania**

ALL-CAR

Not an actual car maker, this firm built conversion units to make a truck out of a car. The mark was filed in 1918, with first use claimed for December 1917.

**Joseph W. Allan,
New York, New York**

LaZal motor trucks first were sold under that name on July 11, 1918, with the trademark application being filed in October of the same year.

**Alma Manufacturing Company,
Alma, Michigan**

Alma Manufacturing Company was a well-known gasoline engine builder, but subsequently entered the motor truck business, with this mark being first used in October 1933, and with a filing date of 1935. The ALCO mark was also used by the American Locomotive Company for their line of automobiles built in the 1905-13 period.

**American La France Fire Engine Company,
Elmira, New York**

Filed on August 4, 1923, this famous manufacturer claimed first use of the mark shown here on January 3, 1921.

Allen Motor Company, Fostoria, Ohio

Built in the 1914-22 period, the Allen resulted from the efforts of E. W. and W. O. Allen. This mark claimed first use in July 1915 and was filed in 1917. About 20,000 Allen cars were built.

Alma Motor Truck Company, Alma, Michigan

REPUBLIC

The famous Republic motor trucks were built for many years, with their Republic trademark being first used in July 1913. At this time the company title was Alma Motor Truck Company.

American Bantam Car Company, Butler, Pennsylvania

In 1930 the American Austin Car Company was established at Butler, Pennsylvania. It retained this name until 1934, and the following year was billed as the American Bantam Car Company. Their trademark application claims November 1, 1936, as the date of first use, with the application being filed in May 1937.

American Bicycle Company, Jersey City, New Jersey

Historians differ as to the precise history of the Waverley automobiles. However, the Waverley trademark was first used in May 1899 and the application was filed in June 1900.

American Bicycle Company, Jersey City, New Jersey

RAMBLER HYDRO CAR

The Rambler trademark was filed in 1901 for "Mechanically-Propelled Vehicles Except Bicycles." The company claimed first use in September 1900. Their Hydrocar trademark was also filed in 1901, with first use in January of that year.

American Motors Corporation, Detroit, Michigan

METROPOLITAN

First used in July 1911 the Metropolitan trademark was not filed by American Motors until February 14, 1957.

American Motors Incorporated, New York, New York

This firm's "AMCO" trademark was first used in February 1916, with the application being filed the following September. Some historians have it that the firm operated from 1917 to 1922; others claim a 1919-20 period.

American Motor Body Corporation, Philadelphia, Pennsylvania

SIX WHEELER

Apparently the Safeway claim to fame was in its automobile passenger buses. American first used the Safeway and Six Wheeler marks in September 1924 and filed trademark applications shortly thereafter.

American Motor Truck Company, Newark, Ohio

In October 1919 American claimed first use of its ACE motor trucks. No other information has been located on this firm.

American Motor Car Company, Indianapolis, Indiana, assignor to American Motors Company, same place.

Filed in December 1905, this trademark was claimed to have been first used on August 1, 1905. Although the beginnings of this firm are sometimes given as 1906, the data accompanying this mark indicate that it was at least a few months earlier.

Frederic A. Ames, Owensboro, Kentucky

THE KENTUCKY THOROUGHBRED

The Kentucky Thoroughbred was an heir in succession to the Ames automobiles. Apparently this model was marketed only for a couple of years, beginning in 1914. The company trademark claimed October 1, 1914, as the first use.

Amplex Manufacturing Company, Detroit, Michigan, assignor to De Soto Motor Corporation, same place.

Our research has come up with no answers concerning the Amplex assignment to De Soto. However, the company claimed first use of this mark on March 30, 1928, and filed the application a month later. For a time the De Soto automobiles achieved record sales within the industry.

Apperson Bros. Automobile Company, Kokomo, Indiana

1

ROADAPLANE

2

Trademark (1) was first used by Apperson on July 15, 1902, even though the application was not filed until February 1919. Trademark (2) for the Roadaplane was filed in May 1916 with the company claiming first use a month earlier. The Roadaplane trademark uses an interesting lettering style, reminiscent of numerous other typefaces of the period.

The O. Armleder Company, Cincinnati, Ohio

The Armleder mark went back to 1884, but no formal application was filed until November 1919. This company built various kinds of wagons, drays, carts, and vehicles (buggies, phaetons, and the like), and later began building automobile-trucks, trailers, and semi-trailers.

Atlas Truck Corporation, York, Pennsylvania

Atlas Worm Drive Merchant's Dispatch trucks were apparently first sold under this title in May 1920, with the trademark application being filed the following January. The "Worm Drive" apparently referred to the rear axle design.

Auburn Automobile Company, Auburn, Indiana

Aurora Automatic Machinery Company, Aurora, Illinois

The Thor motor-propelled vehicles initially included motorcycles. From all appearances, Thor automobiles were manufactured in the 1907-09 period. This beautiful trademark was done in a fancy script, so very popular at the time. In fact, type designers tried to outdo each other in producing highly embellished script faces. Aurora claimed first use of this mark on August 1, 1894.

Auburn was an early player in the automobile business, beginning already in 1900. Curiously, no other Auburn trademarks have appeared except for this Auburn 8 mark first used on December 27, 1932. The application was filed in April 1933.

Automotive Manufacturers Associates, Omaha, Nebraska

BADGER

While not actually an automobile manufacturer, this company produced Badger bodies and cabs for use on truck or automotive chassis, as required. The mark was first used in October 1919.

Austin Motor Company Ltd., Birmingham, England

AUSTIN

Even though the Austin mark is not of American origin, the commonalty of the Austin name merits its inclusion. The company claimed first use of the mark about 1906, and its first use in commerce about 1920. However, the application was not filed in the United States until February, 1958.

Autocar Company, Ardmore, Pennsylvania

AUTOCAR

Autocar

In 1903 Autocar filed for a rather plain looking mark in a gothic face, simply spelling AUTOCAR. The company claimed first use in October 1899. During May 1905 a second trademark application was made, this one in an ornate style, typical of the period.

Atomicar Corporation, Buffalo, New York

ATOMICAR

Claiming first use on July 10, 1947, the Atomicar was a gasoline powered amphibious passenger car. No further information has been located.

Available Truck Company, Chicago, Illinois

1

2

Both of the Available marks were filed on July 10, 1920. However, (1) was first used in May 1910, while the Available Trucks mark (2) was not used until May 1920.

Baker R. & L. Company, Cleveland, Ohio

Baker

1

Even though Baker claimed first use of the Baker trademark (1) in 1898, this particular application was not filed until June 1919. The Owen Magnetic trademarks (2) and (3) were both filed in 1917, with first use claimed as December 1, 1914. Originally the Baker Motor Vehicle Co., the title was changed in 1915 to Baker, Rauch & Lang Co., reflecting a merger at the time (4). Also involved was the R. M. Owen Co., thus the Owen Magnetic marks.

Baker R. & L. Company, Cleveland, Ohio

2

3

4

**Barley Motor Car Company,
Kalamazoo, Michigan**

1

The Roamer trademark (1) was first used on September 14, 1915. At this time the company was at Streator, Illinois, but moved to Kalamazoo in 1917. This mark was filed in 1921. The Pennant mark (2) was first used in March 1923 and was specifically for taxicabs. According to the application, the design is blue with gold staff and words, the concentric circles blue and gold and the background old-ivory color.

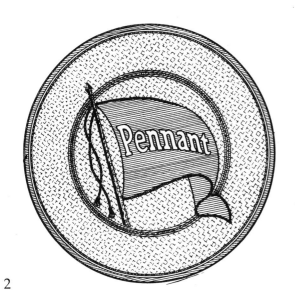

2

**Belmont Motors Corporation,
Lewistown & Harrisburg, Pennsylvania**

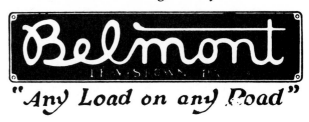

"Any Load on Any Road" described the Belmont automobile-trucks in this 1921 trademark application. The company claimed first use on April 26, 1917.

**Ben-Hur Automobile Company,
Chicago, Illinois**

1

Little information has been found on this company, save for two different trademark applications. Mark (1) was filed in 1916, claiming first use in the previous August. It covered automobiles and motor trucks. Also filed in 1916 was a circular trademark design heralding "form, endurance, and speed." Ben-Hur claimed first use as April 17, 1916.

2

Vincent Bendix, Chicago, Illinois

DUPLEX

The Duplex was an unusual design; the company was actually owned by Bendix Corporation, who also built a car under their own name. The trademark application indicates that it was filed on April 1, 1907. Since it is likely that the vehicle had been fairly well developed prior to filing a trademark application, this seems to put the beginning of production somewhat earlier than the year of 1908 which is generally suggested.

Bentley Motors Ltd., London, England

BENTLEY

This overseas manufacturer first used the Bentley mark in 1919, and in commerce during 1935. Presumably, the latter year was the beginning of regular imports of Bentleys into the United States.

Black Manufacturing Company, Chicago, Illinois

Operating in the 1908-10 period, the Black Crow specifically was built during 1909 and 1910; this resulting from a buyout of the Aurora Motor Works in 1909. The mark was first used in August of that year.

C. H. Blomstrom Motor Company, Detroit, Michigan

QUEEN

Blomstrom first built the Queen, claiming first use of this tradename in August 1903. Among others, this firm also built a car under the Gyroscope tradename, but no application has been found.

Bethlehem Motors Corporation, Allentown, Pennsylvania

This 1918 trademark notes that "the letters of the word are white and the star is emerald green." Covering the Bethlehem trucks, the mark was first used on April 1, 1917.

Frank C. Binkley, Sycamore, Illinois

Some historians state that the Fidelity venture was out of business even before it got started. However, this rather impressive trademark design was applied for on October 1909.

**Bradfield Motors, Inc.,
Wilmington, Delaware and Chicago, Illinois**

**J. G. Brill Company,
Philadelphia, Pennsylvania**

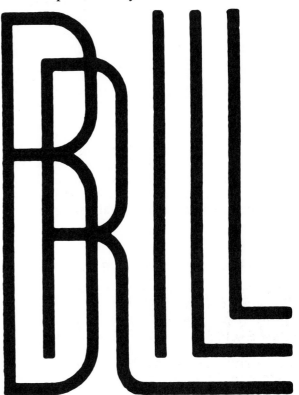

In 1913 this interesting BRILL trademark was first used, although the company did not file an application until 1919. Little reference to this company has been found in the various automotive histories.

Left
This firm operated only for a couple of years, and their application claim of August 20, 1929, as being the first use of the mark tends to establish this date as the enthusiastic, and perhaps, euphoric period of its brief history. Taxicabs seem to have been the extent of the very limited Bradfield production.

**Buckeye Manufacturing Company,
Anderson, Indiana**

In their 1905 application for the Lambert trademark, the company claimed previous use for ten years. The company remained in the automotive field until about 1917. Meanwhile, Lambert was a well-known maker of stationary engines in many different sizes.

**Buckmobile Company,
New Hartford, New York**

BUCKMOBILE

It is usually conceded that this firm operated in the 1903-05 period, although their trademark application lists May 31, 1902, as the first use of the mark.

Buick Motor Company, Flint, Michigan

The famous Buick trademark claimed its first use in January 1904, but the application was not filed until June 1915. W. C. Durant formed General Motors in 1908 and Buick was one of the first members.

L. Burg Carriage Company, Dallas City, Illinois

Buggies, carriages, and spring wagons were in production at this factory as early as 1888. In fact, the company gave that year as the first use of their mark in a 1913 trademark application. However, this also marked the end of automobile production which had begun in 1910.

**Cadillac Auto Truck Company,
Cadillac, Michigan**

The 1915 trademark application for the ACME line indicates that this term was first used by the company on September 22. Our research remains indeterminate as to whether this company was connected with Cadillac Motor Car Company.

**Cadillac Motor Car Company,
Detroit, Michigan**

1

2

In their 1915 trademark application (1), Cadillac claimed 1903 as the first use of the term as applied to automobiles. On August 18, 1905, the company filed for their famous heraldic trademark (2). In their application, it was noted that this mark is: A representation of the coat of arms of Antoine de la Mothe Cadillac, the French explorer, the same comprising a heraldic shield, upon the field of which the heraldry of Cadillac in emblazoned, the shield being surmounted by a crest consisting of a crown, said shield and crest being surrounded by a wreath. Other trademarks appear under the *General Motors* heading.

**Camden Motors Corporation,
Camden, New Jersey**

Although it is generally noted that production of the Frontmobile ended in 1918, their trademark application was not filed until December 30 of that year. Curiously, it was two years earlier, to the day, that the company claimed first use of the mark.

Carvel & Buquor, El Paso, Texas

History has it that the ANAHUAC was an attempt by the Frontenac Motor Company to enter the export car market. This application, filed in April 1922, purports the first use of the mark in August of the previous year. Little other information has been located.

J. I. Case Threshing Machine Company, Racine, Wisconsin

Chalmers Motor Company, Detroit, Michigan

1

Mark (1) of the Chalmers automobiles was filed in 1910. The company began in 1908. Marks (2) and (3) demonstrate a considerable change in trademark design, and this was also evidenced in the design of the car itself. The Chalmers Six and Chalmers Double Six marks were first used June 21, 1915. Trademark (4) was first used in February 1920. By late 1923 production ended.

This famous manufacturer of grain threshers and steam traction engines had a history going back to 1842. In 1910 the company entered the automobile business, claiming the first use of their famous Case Eagle on an automobile as August 1 of that year.

2

Chalmers Motor Company, Detroit, Michigan

3

4

Champion Motors Corporation, Philadelphia, Pennsylvania

Champion first used this trademark in April 1919 and filed their application about a year and a half later. The company lasted into 1924.

Chandler Motor Car Company, Cleveland, Ohio

PIKES PEAK

Chandler was in the automobile business during the 1913-29 period, somewhat longer than many of its competitors. The PIKES PEAK mark shown here was first used October 1, 1922; the application was filed a month later.

**Checker Cab Manufacturing Corporation,
Chicago, Illinois**

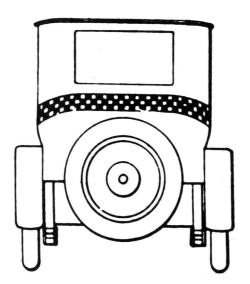

1

This famous company applied for the mark shown here (1) in September 1922, claiming its first use to have been on July 17, 1921. The mark is comprised of a checkered band that substantially encircled the car. The CHECKER mark (2) was first used in October 1928.

Checker Cab Manufacturing Corporation, Chicago, Illinois

2

Louis Chevrolet, Indianapolis, Indiana

FRONTENAC

The FRONTENAC mark was filed in 1925, with first use being claimed for November 1915.

Chevrolet Motor Company, Detroit, Michigan

Chicago Pneumatic Tool Company, Chicago, Illinois

Little Giant

Claiming June 1909 as first use of the Little Giant mark, this application was filed in November 1916. It was for "automobiles and automobile-trucks." No additional data has been located in the various automotive histories at our disposal. This company was well known for its pneumatic tools, as well as large compressors and diesel engines.

Chipman Limited, New York, New York

RHODIA

Outside of this trademark application, filed in 1913, no information has been located on the Rhodia. First use was claimed for November 22, 1911, with automobiles, motorcycles, motor trucks and motor wagons being specifically named.

Chrysler Corporation, Detroit, Michigan

CHRYSLER

1

Organized in 1923, the first mark we have located for Chrysler (1) was first used January 1, 1924.

Left
This famous mark may have been used earlier on Chevrolet automobiles, but has not been located specifically for that purpose. In this instance, the mark was for a combined body polish and cleaner in liquid form. Chevrolet claimed first use on this application as May 9, 1931.

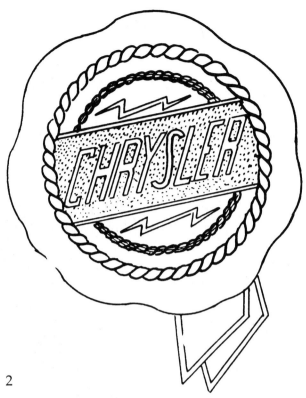

2

3

RED HEAD

4

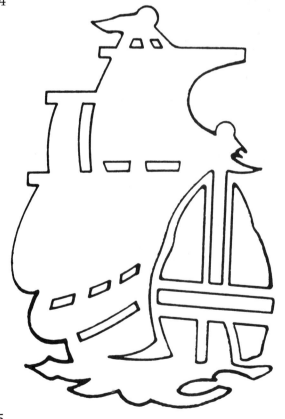

Mark (2) was also first used on this date, with the application for both being filed in February of the same year. The Old English letterform "C" in (3) was for hubcaps and was first used July 1, 1925, while the RED HEAD engine cylinder head trademark was first used in June 1927. Mark (5) was first used June 1, 1928, and (6) was first used in July of the same year.

The IMPERIAL mark (7) was used first on October 27, 1928, as was mark (8). A Chrysler Imperial mark (9) was first used August 2, 1930.

Dodge Brothers marks include (10) first used November 12, 1914; mark (11) of the same first use; and (12) of the same date. Mark (13) for the SENIOR was first used May 10, 1927, and (14) was first used December 17, 1928. Several other marks appear under the *Dodge Brothers* heading.

Two different marks appear in the *Patent Office Gazette* for De Soto, (15) and (16), both first used March 30, 1928.

Mark (17) was issued to Plymouth Motors Corporation and assigned to Chrysler. This mark was first used June 1, 1928.

The Town and Country mark (18) was first used in February 1941, and the Plantation Wagon mark (19) was filed in December 1958.

5

Chrysler Corporation, Detroit, Michigan

6

7

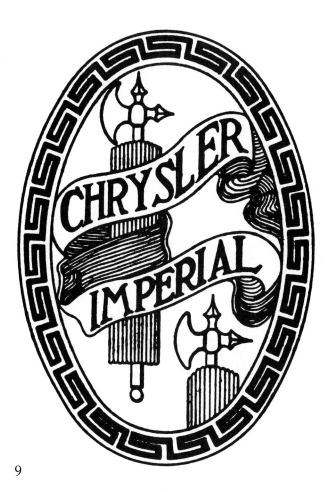

9

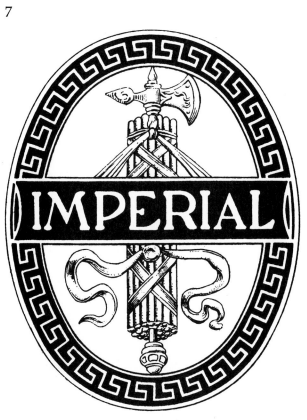

8

10

Chrysler Corporation, Detroit, Michigan

11

12

13

14

DE SOTO

15

DE SOTO

16

Chrysler Corporation, Detroit, Michigan

17

Town and Country

18

PLANTATION *Wagon*

19

**Clark Tructractor Company,
Buchanan, Michigan**

CLARK
TRUCTRACTOR

Although primarily industrial trucks emerged from this firm, it is significant that their CLARK mark shown here was first used in March 1918, with the TRUCTRACTOR mark appearing in December of the following year.

**Classic Motor Car Corporation,
Chicago, Illinois**

Classic claimed this trademark to have been first used June 6, 1916. However, the company was only in business for a short time thereafter, perhaps a year or two.

**Clayton Company, Inc.,
New York, New York**

Apparently this firm limited its efforts to supplying automobile and truck bodies, as well as making carriages and wagons. Filed in November 1919, this mark was first used in January 1915.

**Cleveland Automobile Company,
Cleveland, Ohio**

MILEAGE MOTOR

Those who catalog car manufacturers generally note that a firm under this name operated between 1902 and 1904. However, this mark for "Internal Combustion Engines and Parts Thereof" made the application in 1924, claiming first use to be on September 2 of that year.

**Clinton Motors Corporation,
New York, New York**

**Cole Motor Car Company,
Indianapolis, Indiana**

1

Various automotive histories have it that Cole began building automobiles in 1909. According to mark (1) shown here, the COLE name was first applied thusly in June 1909. Another mark using an eagle and shield design (2) was first used in June 1913.

2

Left
Filed in 1923, this mark was first used October 1, 1922, as applied to the Clinton motor trucks.

Columbia Motors Company, Detroit, Michigan

A number of companies built cars under the Columbia trademark, with this one operating in the 1916-24 period. Curiously, their trademark application of October 1919 lists July 1, 1894, as the first use of the mark, even though the Columbia Six first went on the market in 1917.

Clydesdale Motor Truck Company, Clyde, Ohio

CLYDESDALE

In 1937 Clydesdale applied for this trademark, citing diesel and gasoline motor truck, buses, trailers, and commercial truck bodies as items built under this tradename. The company claimed first use of the mark in October 1915.

Comet Cycle Car Company, Indianapolis, Indiana

Comet Automobile Company, Decatur, Illinois

It is generally agreed that this firm operated in the 1917-22 time period. Technically at least, the company claimed first use of their trademark as May 1, 1916. The application, however, was not filed until January 1920.

Commercial Car Unit Company, Philadelphia, Pennsylvania

KEYSTONE

This truck manufacturer began using the mark shown here on August 29, 1919. No additional information has become manifest during this research project.

Commerce Motor Car Company, Detroit, Michigan

Ostensibly a truck manufacturer, this company also added a large touring car to the 1922 line-up. It was soon discontinued, and the company continued to concentrate on motor trucks. This mark was first used in May 1911, with the application being filed in 1918.

Left
Comet applied for this trademark in December 1913, claiming use since the previous October. The company appears to have lasted for less than a year subsequently.

Commercial Truck Company of America, Philadelphia, Pennsylvania

No additional information outside of this mark has been on the automobiles built by this firm. The trademark application is specifically for automobiles; it was filed in June 1913 and claims first use on June 10, 1910.

Commonwealth Motors Company, Chicago, Illinois

This mark, filed in 1919, had its first use on July 2, 1917. Commonwealth faded by 1922; from its ashes and those of some competitors came the famous Checker taxicabs.

Leonard M. Cotton, Boston, Massachusetts

Cotton concentrated mainly on motor vehicle trailers, automobile bodies, and truck bodies. This mark, filed in 1922, went back to May 15, 1914.

Kenneth Crittenden, Detroit, Michigan (Krit Motor Car Company)

The KRIT lasted from 1909 to about 1916, with this mark being filed in April 1910.

Crosley Corporation, Cincinnati, Ohio

This company, famous for its radios, refrigerators, and other items, began selling cars about 1939. Filed in September 1940, the CROSMOBILE mark claimed first use on September 20 of that year.

Cummins Auto Sales Company, Columbus, Ohio

Operating in the 1915-22 period, this firm claimed first use of the MONITOR trademark as March 1, 1915.

Daniels Motor Car Company, Reading, Pennsylvania

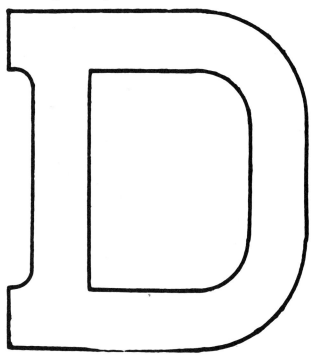

Claiming May 19, 1915, as the first use of the Daniels trademark, the company filed their application in August 1917. This company remained viable until about 1922.

Dart Manufacturing Company, Waterloo, Iowa

Dart appears to have owed at least part of its impetus to William Galloway of Waterloo. The latter owned a sizable mail-order empire. This mark, as applied to motor trucks, appears to have been used as early as 1893, ostensibly to the bicycles being built at the time. This application, filed in July 1913, refers to motor trucks, and likely heralds the beginning of this effort. Apparently, the Dartmobile was a 1922 attempt at passenger cars for this company.

Davis Car Company, Seattle, Washington

In describing this mark, the 1920 application states: "In the drawing the marginal edge is blue and inside same it is red, the letters are white, and the background between the letters is blue." This mark was first used in June 1920.

Dayton Engineering Laboratories Company, Dayton, Ohio

DELCO

Although not an automobile builder, this firm specialized in accessories that included electrical starting, lighting, and ignition systems. The company claimed first use of the DELCO mark in 1911 but did not file the application until 1923.

Delmore Manufacturing Company, New York, New York

Little information can be located on the Parcelmobile from Delmore. The application was filed in 1921, and claims use since June 11, 1919. The description notes that this application was for "small three-wheeled motor vehicles for passengers or freight."

**De Luxe Motor Car Company,
Detroit, Michigan**

Unfortunately, the specific page of the *Patent Office Gazette* was trimmed, including the lower part of this mark. Except for the application being filed on March 1, 1907, we have found no other information.

**Denby Motor Truck Company,
Detroit, Michigan**

This motor truck builder filed the application shown here in October 1914, claiming first use during the previous July.

Denneen Motor Company, Cleveland, Ohio

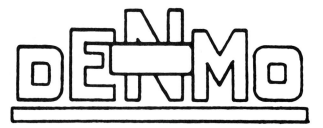

**Dependable Truck & Tractor Company,
Galesburg, Illinois**

DEPENDABLE

Dependable was ostensibly in the farm tractor business, but information in this regard is as scarce as data on their activities in the motor truck scene. This 1920 application lists July 6, 1918, as the first use of the mark for motor trucks.

**Detroit-Dearborn Motor Car Company,
Detroit, Michigan**

In 1910 this company entered the car business, apparently ending the venture the same year. Their application was filed on January 20, 1910.

Left
Information is scarce on the DENMO automobiles, with this 1916 trademark being our only data on the company. Their application is for "automobiles and motor cars, either for pleasure or commercial use."

**Detroiter Motor Car Company,
Detroit, Michigan**

Beginning about 1912 and lasting for some five years, the Detroiter firm spent much of its time reorganizing, and finally went broke. The mark shown here was first used September 1, 1915, with the application being filed the following December.

**Diamond T Motor Car Company,
Chicago, Illinois**

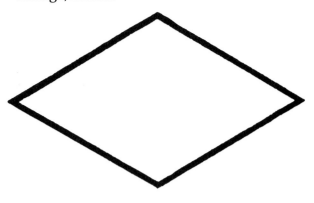

1

Initially, Diamond T built motor cars, as well as trucks. Marks (1) and (2) both claim first use on September 1, 1906, with both being filed on December 8, 1915. Mark (3) claimed first use on March 1, 1918, but this mark was not filed until December 1946. Mark (4) was also filed in 1946, with the company claiming first use as December 1, 1905.

**Diamond Car Sales Corporation,
New York, New York**

A 1923 application lists March 25 of this year as the first use of the GEM trademark. Apparently this firm specialized in auto bodies.

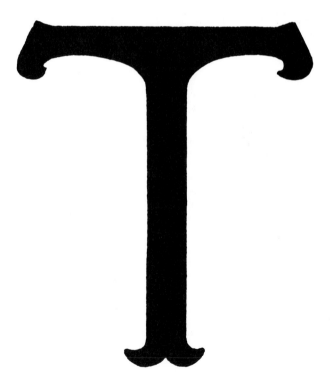

2

**Diamond T Motor Car Company,
Chicago, Illinois**

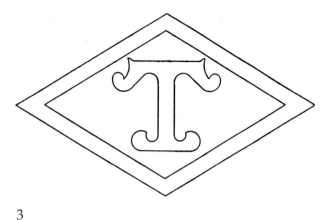

3

4

Diana Motors Company, St. Louis, Missouri

Diana was a subsidiary of Moon Motor Car Company. In the 1925-28 period they built several car models. This mark claimed first use on June 1, 1925.

**Divco-Twin Truck Company,
Detroit, Michigan**

DIVCO-TWIN

Motor Delivery trucks were the subject of this 1938 trademark application. The company claimed first use of DIVCO-TWIN as shown here on November 6, 1935.

**Dixie Motor Car Company,
Louisville, Kentucky**

A 1916 trademark application indicates that the company first used the Dixie Flyer terminology on January 12, 1916. This make was built up to about 1923.

**Dixieland Motor Truck Company,
Texarkana, Texas**

DIXIELAND

July 20, 1918, is stated as the first use of this DIXIELAND trademark, with the company filing the application some twelve months later.

Doble Steam Motors, Emeryville, California

On February 4, 1924, Doble filed this trademark application. The Doble was probably the most technologically advanced steam car ever built, but misfortunes of every sort plagued the company.

Dodge Brothers, Detroit, Michigan

1

Marks (1), (2), and (3), shown here all claim their first use in November 1914. Mark (4) was first used December 7, 1927. Additional marks are shown under the *Chrysler Corporation* heading.

DODGE BROTHERS

2

3

4

Dort Motor Car Company, Flint, Michigan

1

"Own A Dort You Will Like It" reads this trademark, first used in January 1915, (1). A second mark (2) has been located as well; this one having a central background of blue. It was first used in April 1915.

2

Duesenberg Automobile & Motors Company, Indianapolis, Indiana

STRAIGHT

During the 1920-37 period, Duesenberg built some of America's finest cars. This Straight 8 mark was first used November 1, 1920.

Du Pont Motors Incorporated, Wilmington, Delaware

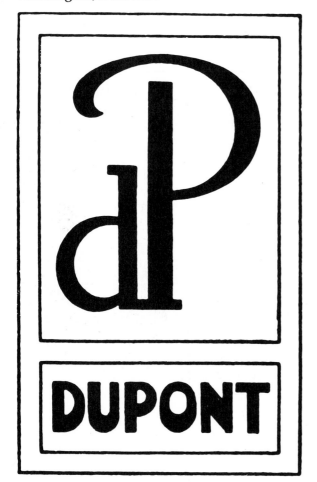

**Durant Motor Company, New York, New York
Durant Motor Company, Elizabeth, New Jersey**

1

The mark shown at (1), with Durant emblazoned over a shield and topped by a griffin, was filed in November 1921. (2) for the Star automobiles was filed in December 1925, with first use being claimed for October of that year.

Left
In the 1919-31 period, this company offered numerous car models. The trademark shown here was first used about November 15, 1919.

Durant Motor Company, New York, New York
Durant Motor Company, Elizabeth, New Jersey

Charles E. Duryea, Reading, Pennsylvania

2

Duryea filed this trademark application in 1905, but our research has not disclosed the length of time the mark had been used prior to the application.

Duffield Motor Company, Des Moines, Iowa

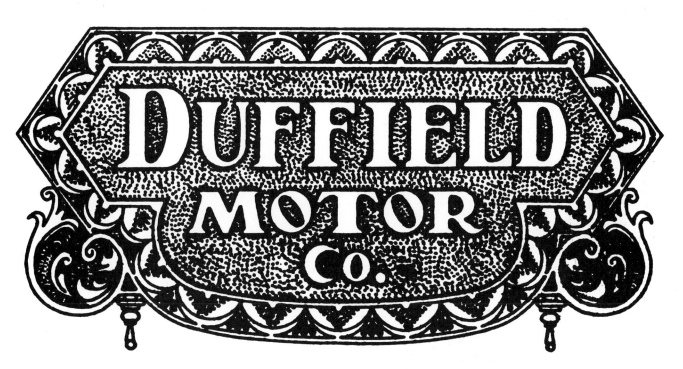

Although automobiles and motor trucks are both listed in this 1928 application, no information has been located as to the activities of the Duffield operation. First use of the mark was claimed as January 18, 1928.

Duty Motor Company, Greenville, Illinois

DUTY

Little information has been found on this company, save for the trademark design shown here. First used in January 1920, application for this mark was filed in the following March.

Eagle Motor Truck Corporation, St. Louis, Missouri

This truck builder filed its Eagle trademark on September 26, 1921, claiming use of it since March 1 of the previous year.

Eclipse Machine Company, Elmira, New York

Although not an automobile manufacturer, Eclipse built automobile transmissions, claiming first use of the mark for this purpose in 1907. Prior to that time, the company had been building bicycles since 1892, and had been building motorcycle transmissions since 1905. This mark was filed December 7, 1914.

Elcar Motor Company, Elkhart, Indiana

Prior to 1915 the cars built were known as Sterling and sold from Elkhart Carriage & Motor Car Company. In 1915 the Elcar appeared, as did the trademark; however, application for this mark was not filed until September 1924.

Electric Vehicle Company, Hartford, Connecticut

1

Columbia electric vehicles apparently began life as early as 1897, enduring until 1913. The Columbia mark shown at (1) 1905. The intricate script design of the mark was typical of the period. At (2), three other marks are shown, two of them being for Columbia motor boats.

**Electric Vehicle Company,
Hartford, Connecticut**

Columbia

Columbia

2

**Elkhart Carriage & Motor Car Company,
Elkhart, Indiana**

ELCAR

The ELCAR mark has been previously noted under that company name, with this earlier mark from Elkhart. First use of this one was on December 14, 1915.

**Empire Automobile Company,
Indianapolis, Indiana**

Claiming first use of the Empire mark on August 1, 1909, this company continued at Indianapolis until 1912 and moved to Pennsylvania, operating there under Greenville Metal Products.

**Electric and Ordnance Accessories Co.,
Ltd., Birmingham, England**

STELLITE

Although this book does not include *every* foreign auto builder, this one seemed interesting because of the unusual tradename, and because it was filed already in 1914. The company claimed first use in July of the previous year.

**Erskine Engineering Company,
Jacksonville, Florida**

Claiming first use as February 1, 1921, Erskine applied this mark to "automobile parts and accessories." There is no apparent connection to the Erskine automobiles built by Studebaker.

Elgin Motor Car Company, Chicago, Illinois

This firm operated for a decade, ending in 1925. Their interesting, and rather attractive trademark was first used September 20, 1915.

Essex Motors, Detroit, Michigan

ESSEX

1

Although automotive historians generally ascribe 1919 as the beginning of production for the Essex, mark (1) and mark (2) shown here both claim September 21, 1917, as their date of first use. Mark (1) was filed in November 1918, and mark (2) was filed in November 1922.

Everitt-Metzger-Flanders Company, Detroit, Michigan

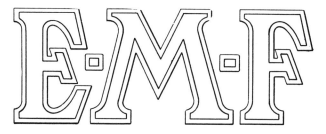

Operating in the 1908-12 period, the E-M-F was marketed by Studebaker. This mark was filed in 1909.

2

FWD Corporation, Clintonville, Wisconsin

FWD

1

This firm claimed first use of mark (1) as July 14, 1911, applying it to trucks, fire engines, and the like. The Rough Neck mark (2) was first used August 5, 1954.

ROUGH NECK

2

**Fairbanks, Morse & Company,
Chicago, Illinois**

FARMOBILE

Fairbanks-Morse has been, and remains famous as a builder of internal combustion engines. Relatively unknown though, is the company's excursion into the automobile business. This mark, filed in 1906, indicates the intended sales arena for the Farmobile.

**Falls Motors Corporation,
Sheboygan Falls, Wisconsin**

Fargo Motor Corporation, Detroit, Michigan

The Fargo Express mark was applied to "motor trucks and buses. . ." and was filed in April 1928, barely a month after the company claimed first use of the mark.

**Farmers Union State Exchange,
Omaha, Nebraska**

Concentric circles enclosing various tillage tools make this a rather unique trademark, especially as applied to motor trucks. First used in November 1917, the mark was filed in February 1920.

Left
While production of the Falls automobiles is generally considered to be in the 1922-24 period, this mark claims first use in January 1903 for "automobiles, trucks or trailers for automobiles, and Autotrucks." The mark was filed in September 1916, somewhat ahead of the suggested production period.

**Federal Motor Truck Company,
Detroit, Michigan**

FEDERAL

1

Mark (1) for Federal indicates that it was first used on July 15, 1910, although it was not filed until February 1913. Mark (2) for the Federal Fast Express was first used on July 26, 1922, with the trademark application being filed a month later.

FEDERAL *Fast Express*

2

Joseph B. Ferguson, New York, New York

FERGUS

This company claimed first use of the mark in May 1915, announcing a manufacturing facility at Newark, New Jersey. Due to curtailments because of the World War, production did not begin until about 1920.

Fisher Body Corporation, Detroit, Michigan

This famous company claimed first use of the mark shown here on August 1, 1922, and filed their trademark application the same month.

Ford Motor Company, Dearborn, Michigan

1

Mark (1), filed in 1915, shows the Ford script mark, claiming first use as February 15, 1895; mark (2) was essentially the same, except that it was for "plate glass and lenses." Mark (3) is a 1956 renewal.

2

FORD

3

4

Ford Motor Company, Dearborn, Michigan

Ford

5

Mark (4) of March 1912 is a somewhat different design than previously used; mark (5) is for Ford lubricating oils and was first used on August 14, 1925. Mark (6), filed in August 1928, applies since November 1927 to shock absorbers; January 1, 1928 on bumpers; October 23, 1925, on airplanes; and February 15, 1895, on a variety of other items, including gasoline tanks, springs, radiators, luggage carriers, and tire carriers.

Mark (7) is a Lincoln mark, first used August 3, 1920; mark (8) was first used September 15, 1936, and was filed in January 1940. Another Ford script mark (9) was filed in 1941; it claimed first use on October 1, 1934, for "electric lighters for cigars and cigarettes." The Ford script mark (10) was first used in connection with "radio receiving sets and parts thereof" on September 19, 1932; this mark was filed in October 1937.

6

LINCOLN

7

Lincoln Zephyr

8

Ford

9

Ford

10

FALCON

11

Victoria

12

41

Ford Motor Company, Dearborn, Michigan

FORD-MERCURY
MERCURY

13

The Falcon mark (11) was first used January 23, 1959, while the Victoria mark (12) was first used January 1, 1930. However, the application for this mark was not filed until February 1953.

Mercury and Ford-Mercury marks (13) were filed on August 8, 1938, with first use being claimed for the first day of that month. Also claiming first use for that day was the Ford-Mercury mark of (14). On November 22, 1938, first use was claimed for the Mercury 8 trademark of (15); this mark was filed in December of that year.

MERCURY

15

MONARCH
METEOR

16

Continental

17

FORD

MERCURY

14

18

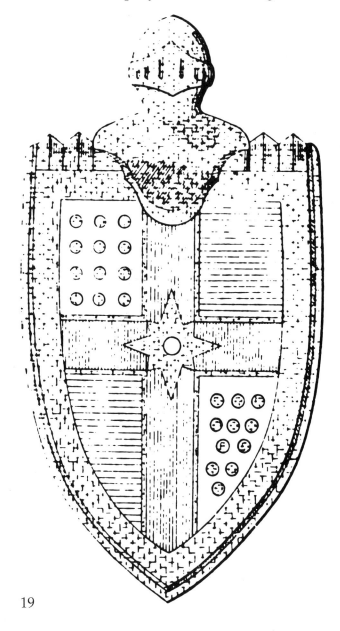

19

21

The Monarch and Meteor marks (16) were filed in January 1960, with a notation that the Monarch was a Canadian registration of 1945, and the Meteor a similar registration of 1948. September 20, 1940, was the first use of the Continental mark (17) shown here; mark (18) was first used October 3, 1941. A detailed explanation of (19) accompanies this February 1946 application: "The drawing is lined for color: the helmet borders, roundels and star being gold, the cross red, and the quarters blue and white." First use was claimed for January 11, 1946. Mark (20) was first used November 18, 1949; the application notes that, "The drawing is lined for color: the border, roundels and lions being silver, the inverted "Y" black, and the three triangular sections red, blue, and grey, respectively." Mark (21) was for forgings and stampings, with November 1948 being claimed as the first use. Essentially the same mark (22) was used beginning in November 1948 for automobiles, trucks, buses, vehicle parts and accessories. Mark (23) for independent wheel suspensions claimed first use on June 18, 1948.

The Ford Consul mark (24) filed in 1952 claimed first use in October 1950. January 27, 1952, was claimed as first use for Monterey (25). The Ranch Wagon (26), Country Sedan (27), and Courier (28) all were first used February 1, 1952, with the Capri (29) following on February 6. During November 1953 the Skyliner trademark (30) was first used.

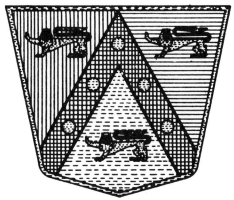

20

22

Hydra-Coil

23

CONSUL

24

MONTEREY

25

RANCH WAGON

26

COUNTRY SEDAN

27

COURIER

28

Ford Motor Company, Dearborn, Michigan

CAPRI

29

Skyliner

30

Thunderbird

31

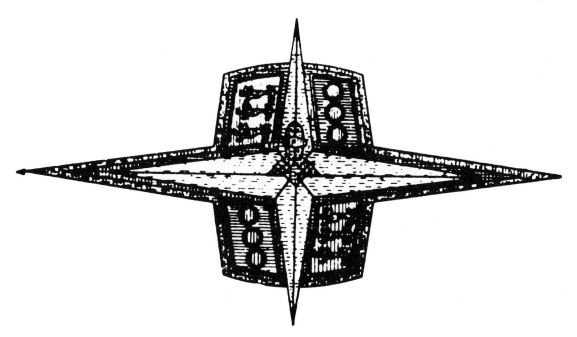

32

Ford Motor Company, Dearborn, Michigan

Fairlane

33

MONTCLAIR

34

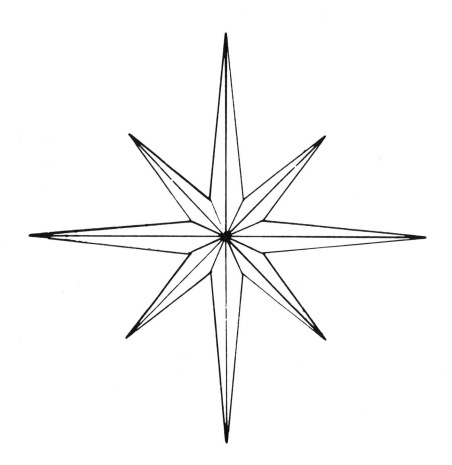

35

Mark (31) claimed first use February 20, 1954; mark (32) shows first use of September 14, 1954. The application notes that, "the drawing is lined for color, the outer border being gold, the inner border being black, the cross being silver, the lions being gold and their background being red, the roundels being gold with red centers and their background being blue and the helmet and armor being gold." The Fairlane mark of (33) shows first use of November 12, 1954; the Montclair mark of (34) claiming first use of December 2, 1954.

PREMIERE

36

Parklane

37

TURNPIKE CRUISER

38

CORSAIR

39

CITATION

40

Mark (35) was first used September 14, 1955; the Premier mark of (36) was first used September 16 of that year. The Parklane mark (37) was first used in August 1955.

Turnpike Cruiser, as shown at (38), was first used February 7, 1956; the Corsair mark (39) was first used on the following April 16. June 14, 1956, was cited as first use of the Citation (40) and Pacer (41) marks, with the Comet mark shown at (42) coming on June 26 of the same year. The Roundup mark (43) shows first use of July 18, 1956, as does the Ranger mark

PACER

41

COMET

42

ROUNDUP

43

RANGER

44

RANCHERO

45

COLONY PARK

46

COMMUTER

47

VOYAGER

48

GREEN LIGHT

49

VILLAGER

50

January 18, 1957, was claimed as first use of the Ranchero mark (45), with the Colony Park (46) and Commuter (47) marks being first used February 13 of that year. Then, on February 22, came first use of the Voyager trademark (48). Green Light (49) was for automobiles and also appears to have been applied to reconditioned used automobiles. It was first used July 10, 1957. The Villager mark (50) was first used on September 4 of that year.

In 1958 the Marauder mark (51) appears, with first use claimed as January 2. Mark (52) claims first use as October 27, 1959; it was filed the following December.

Mark (53) was filed by the Ford Motor Sales Company, Dearborn, Michigan, on July 18, 1936, and claims first use as July 5, 1935.

MARAUDER

51

52

53

**Fort Pitt Motor Mfg. Co., Inc.,
New Kensington, Pennsylvania**

Operating in the 1909-11 period, Fort Pitt applied for their Pittsburgh Six trademark on November 2, 1908.

**H. H. Franklin Mfg. Company,
Syracuse, New York**

This application of June 30, 1906, was for the famous Franklin automobiles. The outstanding script design typified the mood of the times. Franklin operated in the 1901-34 period.

Gambill Motor Company, Chicago, Illinois

Gardner Motor Company, St. Louis, Missouri

Generally acknowledged to have been in operation from 1920 to 1931, this Gardner mark claimed first use on January 10, 1920. The mark was "displayed in white on a red field having an irregular border of white."

Garford Motor Truck Company, Lima, Ohio

1

Beginning as an automobile builder (1), this firm eventually concentrated on motor trucks (2) and buses (3). The Greyhound mark shown here was first used July 9, 1925 and was filed in March of the following year.

Left
An application of May 1928 claims use of this Blue Ribbon trademark since the previous April 18. However, since the firm does not appear in the various automotive histories a question arises as to the nature of their activities.

Garford Motor Truck Company, Lima, Ohio

2

3

**General Motors Corporation,
Detroit, Michigan**

1

Oldsmobile

2

OLDSMOBILE

3

BUICK

4

BUICK

5

Left

The General Motors trademarks include marks from many different companies; additional marks may also be found under specific company headings prior to their acquisition by General Motors.

Mark (1) was first used December 1900 by Oldsmobile; it was filed in 1924. Mark (2) was first used in December 1900 and was filed at the same time as (1) above. Filed in 1926, mark (3) was first used in 1900 as well.

January 2, 1904, is listed as the date of first use for the Buick mark (4); the same holds true for marks (5) and (6). While the latter two marks were filed in September 1924, mark (4) was not filed until September 20, 1947.

**General Motors Corporation,
Detroit, Michigan**

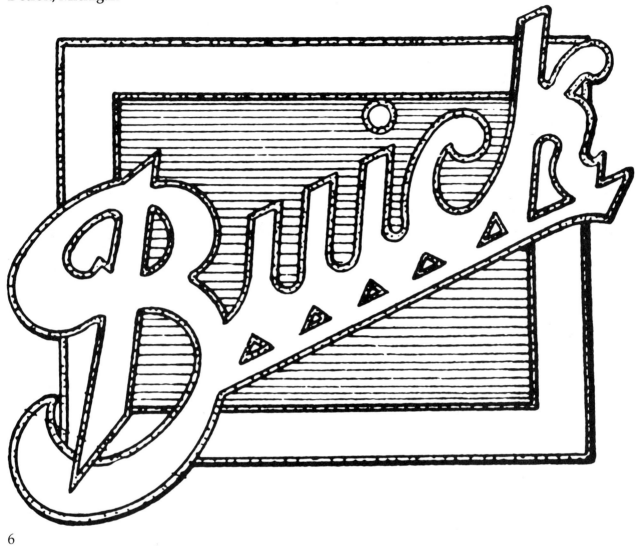

6

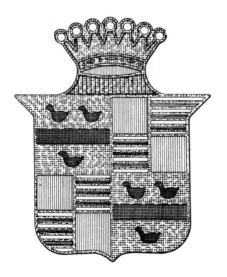

7

The Cadillac mark shown in (7) was first used September 1, 1902. It was followed by mark (8) of 1903. Both were filed in 1924. General Motors claimed first use of the Fleetwood mark (9) in January 1909 for automobile bodies. This mark was filed in 1947.

Mark (10) was first used August 1, 1911, and covered "motor-driven trucks." It was filed in 1924. Marks (11) and (12) are virtually identical except that they covered different components. Mark (11) was "for motor vehicles, not including engines and structural parts therefor . . ." and mark (12) was "for truck and coach parts. . . ." These two marks were filed in 1954.

General Motors Corporation,
Detroit, Michigan

CADILLAC

8

Fleetwood

9

10

11

General Motors Corporation,
Detroit, Michigan

12

13

14

General Motors Corporation,
Detroit, Michigan

OAKLAND

15

16

In 1924, application was made for marks (13) and (14), both of which saw first use in 1913. Mark (14) specifically notes that "the main . . . portion of the mark is blue in color, the letters and the marginal band being white, and the narrow border bands about the letters and about the white border band (which are formed by dams which prevent the blue and white enamels from mingling) being the color of the metallic plate on which the mark appears, or silver color in the facsimiles submitted."

The Oakland marks of (15) and (16) were filed in September 1924. Mark (15) claimed first use of February 1908, while mark (16) was first used in February 1916. The application also notes that "the letters constituting the word 'Oakland' and the upper and lower panels of the oval shield being lined to indicate the color blue, as such parts are blue in the trademark as actually used."

Mark (17) was filed in March 1926 and was first used on December 17 of the previous year. Mark (18) was likewise filed in 1926, claiming first use on the exact same date as mark (17) above. The Oakland mark of (19) was first used July 1, 1925, with the application being filed later that same year. The lining in the panel indicates the color blue, as actually used.

General Motors Corporation,
Detroit, Michigan

17

PONTIAC

18

19

20

On August 7, 1926, mark (20) was first used; it was filed in January 1927. The La Salle mark (21) was first used on August 7, 1926, with an application being filed the following October. This mark notes that "the trademark consists of the word 'La Salle,' the same being the last part of the name of the celebrated French explorer René Robert Cavelier, Sieur de La Salle." Mark (22) was first used in August 1926, with the application being filed the following October.

General Motors Corporation,
Detroit, Michigan

21

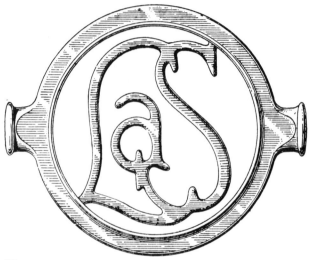

22

23

24

The Viking mark shown in (23) was first used December 31, 1928, with the application being filed the following April. In the application it is noted that "the drawing is lined to indicate the colors yellow and black, although color is disclaimed as a part of the mark."

A distinctive combination of red and blue, together with gold color was used in this Oakland mark (24); it was first used June 22, 1928. The Oldsmobile mark shown at (25) was first used on January 4, 1928, and application was made the following March. In (26) we see the Marquette mark. First used and filed in May 1929 the application states that, "no claim is made to the use of the word 'Marquette' except as the word is associated with other features of the mark in the manner illustrated in the drawing. The drawing is lined to indicate the colors red and black."

25

26

27

28

I. C. V.

29

Mark (27) was first used in December 1929 but was not filed until March 1948. In contrast, the Pontiac mark (28) was first used and was filed in January 1931. It was for "automobiles and motor-driven trucks . . ." The I. C. V. mark (29) was for ventilating windows for automobiles, buses, and trucks. It was lined to indicate the color red, although the color was not an essential feature of the trademark. This mark was first used on November 22, 1932, and was filed the following month. Likewise, the Fisher I. C. V. mark (30) was first used and was filed on the same dates as (29) above.

The GM mark (31) was limited to repair and replacement parts of motor vehicles in this specific application. It claimed first use of September 15, 1933, and was filed on February 28, 1934. GM filed the Master trademark (32) in December 1936, claiming first use on November 13 of that year. In August 1937 the La Salle mark shown in (33) was filed, claiming first use on the previous July 20.

**General Motors Corporation,
Detroit, Michigan**

30

GM

31

MASTER

32

La Salle

33

Fleetline

34

DYNAFLOW

35

Silver Streak

36

As noted at various points in this book, it is an interesting study to observe the changes in trademark designs over the years. Those of the early part of the century often used florid designs, typical of the period. By the 1920s, the script faces and detailed designs had given way to simple, bold designs, reminiscent of Puritan austerity coupled to Yankee ruggedness. However, by 1940 script faces were again becoming popular, as evidenced by this Fleetline mark (34) filed in March 1941. GM claimed first use on the preceding January 14.

General Motors Corporation,
Detroit, Michigan

OLDSMOBILE ROCKET

37

38

Automotive manufacturing virtually ceased during World War II. Since there were no cars being built, there was little need to cast about for new trademarks. Thus, there is a dearth of trademark progress during this period. Subsequent to World War II, this pent-up activity resulted in many new models, and many new trademarks. One of these is the Dynaflow mark (35). It was first used December 27, 1947, and was filed the following April. This mark was for "complete power transmission units for motor vehicles . . ." The Silver Streak mark (36) was first used January 15, 1948, and was filed the following October. Oldsmobile Rocket (37) automobile engines first got this name officially on November 16, 1948, although the application was not filed until July 1952. With this mark, as well as for numerous others, there are similar and/or related marks which may or may not appear in this book. Despite the thousands of hours of research, it is entirely possible to have gone past some marks.

**General Motors Corporation,
Detroit, Michigan**

Le Sabre

39

Corvette

40

FLAME BIRD

41

FIRE BIRD

42

STAR CHIEF

43

In June 1950 General Motors filed this "OK" mark (38) for used automobiles and trucks. The company claimed first use of July 1949 on the mark as shown, and since 1929 on the letters "OK." The Le Sabre mark (39) was first used on July 16, 1951, with an application being filed in March 1952. January 9, 1953, was claimed as the date of first use for the Corvette mark (40). This application was filed the following March. The Flame Bird mark (41) was first used November 19, 1953, and was filed the following December; the Fire Bird mark (42) has the same first use and filing dates. In December 1953 General Motors applied for this Star Chief mark (43), claiming December 8 of that year as the first use.

General Motors Corporation,
Detroit, Michigan

EL CAMINO

44

CORVAIR

45

Strato Streak

46

47

El Camino was first used in January 1954 "for automotive vehicles—-namely, trucks." This mark (44) was filed in March 1958. Corvair (45) was a term first used in or before January 1954, although the application was not filed until August 6, 1959. Another mark of this time period was the Strato Streak (46) for internal combustion engines and parts thereof. It was first used August 30, 1954, and was filed the following October. Another Corvette mark (47) was first used January 29, 1955, and filed in December 1956.

General Motors filed the application for the Cameo mark (48) in January 1958 "for trucks." It was first used March 25, 1955. The Seville mark (49) was first used August 26, 1955, with the application being filed on September 1 of that year. The famous Impala trademark claimed first use on January 18, 1956; this mark was filed on June 27 of the following year. A Viking mark (51) was filed in April 1957 "for trucks." First use was claimed as March 21, 1957. Also see mark (23) previously shown.

**General Motors Corporation,
Detroit, Michigan**

CAMEO

48

SEVILLE

49

IMPALA

50

VIKING

51

YEOMAN

52

FLEETSIDE

53

BROOKWOOD

54

HI-THRIFT

55

INVADER

56

A Yeoman trademark (52) for automobiles was applied for on June 27, 1957, with first use being claimed for April 30 of that year. GM applied for this Fleetside mark (53) in November 1957, with first use claimed for September 17 of that year. The Brookwood mark (54) was first used in April 1957; application for this mark was filed the following June. Hi-Thrift internal combustion engines were the subject of the mark shown at (55). Filed in August 1958, it was first used on July 11 of that year. Invader was the subject of this mark (56) "for automobiles." Filed in April 1959, this mark claimed first use on the previous February 19. Mark (57) was for "automotive hardware and trim . . ." with September 3, 1959, being the first application of the

mark to mouldings. This was filed in October 1959. The Parkwood mark (58) was first used in February 1958, and an application for it was filed a month later.

As has been pointed out in the introduction to this book, this listing of trademarks may not contain *every* trademark of *every* automotive manufacturer. In some cases, tradenames were never filed, and in others, we could easily have missed them, despite using the annual indexes and looking at every page. Again, we emphasize that these marks are presented solely in a historic context; in that light, they provide a valuable historic record concerning their origins.

**General Motors Corporation,
Detroit, Michigan**

57

PARKWOOD

58

Charles W. Gillette, Chicago, Illinois

"Motor Trucks and Automobiles" were claimed for this Lakeside trademark of Gillette. Filed on April 1, 1916, the company claimed first use on the previous February 26. Since the various automotive histories are without comment on this firm, it is presumed that their major activities were in the motor truck field.

Eugene Goldman, Chicago, Illinois

MASTER

1

The Master trademark was first used by Goldman for "motor trucks and automobiles" in November 1916. The following January, application was made for mark (1). Motor trucks were described in the application for the mark (2) covering the Eugol trucks. This one was first used May 5, 1921, and application was made the following March. Thus, it is a virtual certainty that the company remained in the truck manufacturing business for at least a few years.

2

Graham Brothers, Evansville, Indiana

1

Left
Graham Brothers specialized in motor trucks. Our research located mark (1) as the earliest trademark, with first use being claimed as January 2, 1920. In March following, the application was filed. Mark (2) shows Graham Brothers Detroit, although no claim was made for the word "Detroit" apart from the mark. First use was claimed as September 28, 1922, and the application was filed the following November. G-Boy as a tradename of Graham Brothers came into being April 1, 1926, and was specifically for "trucks and constructive parts thereof."

Graham Brothers, Evansville, Indiana

2

3

Goodyear Tire & Rubber Company, Akron, Ohio

Nothing has been located in the various automotive histories concerning good years activities in the automobile and truck business. Yet, this trademark, filed in November 1920, defines "automobiles and motor trucks" as the subject of activity. This mark was first used thus on February 26, 1920.

Graham-Paige Motors Corporation, Dearborn, Michigan

1

Operating for the 1927-41 period, Graham-Paige applied form mark (1) and mark (2) on the same date, January 6, 1930. Likewise, both marks claimed the same first date of use, December 31, 1929. Mark (1) is for the Paige Commercial Car, while mark (2) is for "automobiles and constructive parts thereof."

**Graham-Paige Motors Corporation,
Dearborn, Michigan**

2

2

3

Presumably, the various marks shown here are related to one another. However, mark (1) is shown under Benjamin A. Gramm, Chillicothe, Ohio; this mark was filed July 25, 1905. Mark (2) for the Gramm-Logan trucks was filed December 13, 1909, it being noted in the application that the mark "consists of the words Gramm Logan in the handwriting of Benjamin A. Gramm." With this application, the company address is shown as Bowling Green, Ohio.

Mark (3) for the Gramm-Bernstein "automobiles and motor trucks" was filed in 1920, with first use claimed for June 1914. With this application, Gramm-Bernstein was located at Lima, Ohio. No details can be located on the Pioneer mark (4), ostensibly for automobiles. This mark was applied for by the Gramm-Bernstein folks in November 1919, even though the mark showed first use of February 8, 1917. Gramm Motors Inc. applied for mark (5) in May 1927, noting first use of October 1, 1926.

Gramm Motors Inc., Lima, Ohio

"THAT CAR OF QUALITY"

1

4

5

6

Grant Motor Car Corporation, Cleveland, Ohio

Although most automotive histories indicate that the Grant Six was built in the 1912-13 period, this mark did not claim first use until January 16, 1914, and was not filed until May 11, 1920.

Greenville Mfg. Company, Greenville, Ohio

Beginning September 1, 1923, the Omort trademark was applied to motor-driven dump trucks. Greenville Mfg. Company applied for this trademark in October 1923.

Greyhound Motors Corporation, New York, New York

Gray Motor Corporation is generally stated to have operated in the 1922-26 period. However, this mark, filed in December 1921, claimed first use as May 1920. Possibly this is because of numerous delays in getting the car into production.

H.C.S. Motor Car Company, Indianapolis, Indiana

The initials were those of Harry C. Stutz, who had begun building cars in 1911. H.C.S. operated in the 1920-25 period, with this trademark being first used on November 15, 1919.

Left
With their trademark application of March 18, 1920, Greyhound staked out their application of this mark to "automobile bodies and frames." First use was claimed for September 10, 1919.

H.P.M. Motors, Incorporated,
New York, New York

H.P.M. appears to have been a marketing organization, rather than a manufacturer; various automotive historians note that the car was actually built by Moller Motor Car Company, Lewistown, Pennsylvania. The Falcon trademark was first used November 23, 1921, and was filed a few days later.

Hamilton Motors Company,
Grand Haven, Michigan

PANHARD

1

Hamilton began building cars in 1917, with the Panhard trademark (1) claiming first use on March 1 of that year. The company also built motor trucks and stayed in business into the early 1920s, apparently dropping from sight in 1921. Mark (2) is for their Apex Twin-Frame Truck; first use for this mark was claimed as September 1, 1919.

2

Hanson Motor Company,
Atlanta, Georgia

The Hanson trademark was filed in May 1920 and was first used in February 1917. This company operated into 1925.

Harroun Motors Corporation,
New York, New York

1

**Harroun Motors Corporation,
New York, New York**

2

The Harroun was built by Ray Harroun, winner of the first Indianapolis 500 race in 1911. Harroun Motors operated in the 1917-22 period, with mark (1) claiming first use on January 1, 1917. Mark (2) claims first use as January 3 of that year.

**Hatfield Motor Vehicle Company,
Cortland, New York**

Various automotive histories note that Miamisburg, Ohio, was the home of the Buggyabout, with the Cortland address being the location where it was developed. It was built in the 1907-08 time frame. This mark was filed on May 20, 1907.

James A. Hayes, New York, New York

The Legion taxicab does not appear in the automotive histories we have researched, and perhaps this company limited its activities to building taxicab bodies, or perhaps to converting motor cars to taxicabs. The Legion mark was first used March 31, 1925, with the application appearing the following September.

**Harvey Motor Truck Company,
Harvey, Illinois**

Little information has been found during our research on the Harvey, except for this single trademark, claiming first use of November 1, 1918. The mark was filed in May of the following year.

Hayes-Diefenderfer Company, New York, New York

HayDee

The HayDee trademark applied to "extensions for automobile chassis, also automobile bodies and automobile windshield, dashes and springs." First used on May 15, 1917, this mark might well be related to the James A. Hayes mark above. However, we have found no evidence in either direction.

Haynes Automobile Company, Kokomo, Indiana

2

1

Mark (1) claimed first use of this design in 1907, although the application was not filed until 1919. Mark (2) denoting "America's First Car" claimed first use on June 25, 1912. Actually, Elwood Haynes had built his first car in 1894, thus the claim. The company endured until 1925.

Hebb Motors Company, Lincoln, Nebraska

PATRIOT

None of our research efforts have yielded additional information on the Patriot except for this mark. It claimed first use on October 1, 1917, the mark being filed the following February.

Heil Company, Milwaukee, Wisconsin

R.F.C

1

Heil was an early manufacturer of truck bodies, with these six different marks all claiming first use in May 1919. Thus, Heil has been a leader in this specialized field for many years.

Heil Company, Milwaukee, Wisconsin

R. S. C.

2

S. F. C.

3

S. S. C.

4

2 IN I

5

3 IN I

6

76

Henney Motor Company, Freeport, Illinois

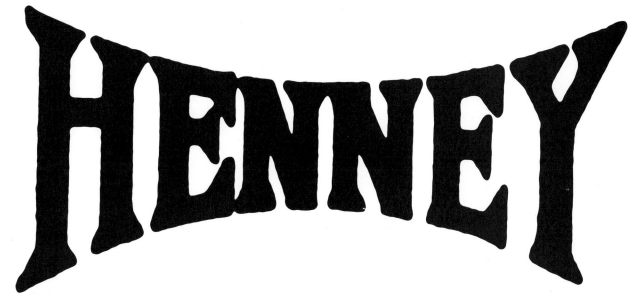

1

Henney is not so well known for its automobiles (1921-31) as for its hearses and ambulances, the latter being built up to 1954. Mark (1) claims first use as 1916, although the application for this mark was not filed until February 20, 1952. Mark (2) is for the Leveldraulic design of Henney hearses, ambulances, and other vehicles. It was first used May 3, 1937.

LEVELDRAULIC

2

**Holcomb & Hoke Mfg. Company,
Indianapolis, Indiana**

BUTTER-KIST SHOP

This company was not an automobile manufacturer, but instead, built special truck bodies, technically described as a "food and beverage dispensing automobile truck." This mark was first used February 1, 1926.

Highway Motors Company, Chicago, Illinois

Highway Knight motor trucks began using this trademark design in May 1919. Little else has been ascertained regarding the firm.

Hopper Auto Sales Company, New Rochelle, New York

The HopFord was one of the many conversion devices intended to render the family car into the family farm tractor or perhaps as a light truck. The mark claims first use March 1, 1918.

Hol-Tan Company, New York, New York

This Hol-Tan trademark was filed May 12, 1906, about the same time that the company became established as an automobile dealer. A Hol-Tan automobile was built in 1908.

Holmes Automobile Company, Canton, Ohio

The Holmes air-cooled design ran from 1918 to 1923, with this mark first being used February 8, 1921.

Harry S. Houpt, New York, New York

The Houpt first appeared in 1909, and the following year as the Houpt-Rockwell the latter disappearing by 1911. This mark was filed January 19, 1909.

Hudford Company of Chicago, Chicago, Illinois

The Fitzall was a conversion unit "for making motor trucks from automobiles." Hudford claimed first use for this mark as June 15, 1919.

Hudson Motor Car Company, Detroit, Michigan

HUDSON

1

Hudson began building cars in 1909 with marks (1), (2), (3), and (4) all pointing to that fact. Mark (5) was for the Dover gasoline trucks from Hudson; this mark claimed first use on June 7, 1929. Mark (6) was for the Sunsedan automobile bodies; it was first used on November 7 of 1929.

2

HUDSON
3

HUDSON
4

5

The Hudson 8 trademark (7) was first used January 9, 1930, and mark (8) was first used August 19, 1937. The Hudson Terraplane mark (9) was likewise first used on August 19, along with mark (10) of the same date. Hudson first used the Autoplano mark (11) on September 16, 1932, and the Hudson Weathermaster automobile heaters (utilizing heat from the engine) first saw use of this mark (12) on October 13, 1939.

Mark (13) was first used in October 1945, and the H-145 mark (14) referring to internal combustion engines was first used September 21, 1950. The Hudson Jet mark (15) was first used in December 1952, as was mark (16) and mark (17). The Hudson Hornet mark (18) shown here was first used on September 21, 1950.

**Hudson Motor Car Company,
Detroit, Michigan**

SUNSEDAN

6

7

9

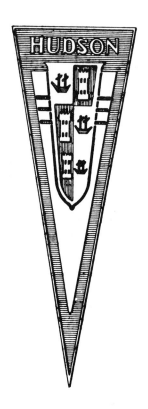

8

10

Hudson Motor Car Company,
Detroit, Michigan

AUTOPLANO

11

HUDSON

WEATHERMASTER

12

13

H-145

14

**Hudson Motor Car Company,
Detroit, Michigan**

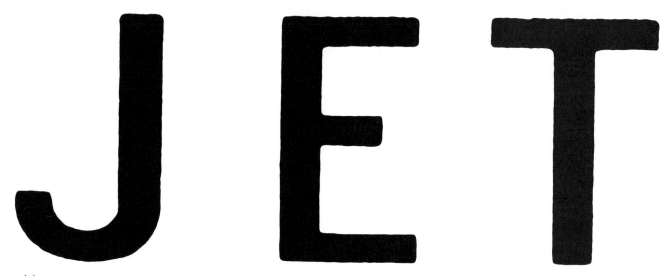

15

16

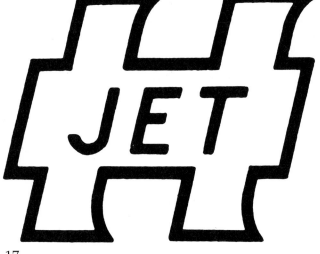

17

Hupp Motor Car Company, Detroit, Michigan

1

This company operated in the 1909-41 period, with mark (1) denoting November 10, 1908, as the first use of the Hupmobile trademark. In July 1915 the company also adopted mark (2). It simply represented a typographical change, reflecting the shift from the ornate script face of earlier years to a more contemporary design.

Hupp Motor Car Company, Detroit, Michigan

Hupmobile

2

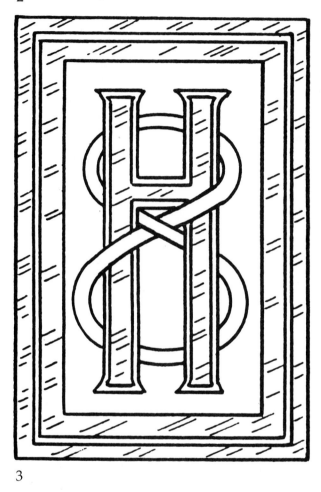

3

Ideal Motor Car Company, Indianapolis, Indiana

Ideal was a company organized by Harry C. Stutz. Their 1912 trademark application was for "automobiles, trucks, and similar vehicles." The company claimed first use of this mark as April 2, 1911.

Illinois Auto Truck Company, Chicago, Illinois

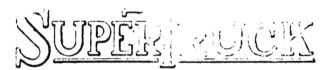

Unfortunately, this SuperTruck trademark was printed very poorly in the *Patent Office Gazette*. It was for motor trucks and trailers, with first use claimed for March 1, 1919.

Ideal Auto Company, Fort Wayne, Indiana

Left
Ideal noted "automobiles and auto-trucks" in describing the goods covered by their 1911 trademark application. The company appears to have specialized in motor trucks, building them until 1915. This mark was claimed for first use in August 1908.

**Illinois Diamond Cab Company,
Chicago, Illinois**

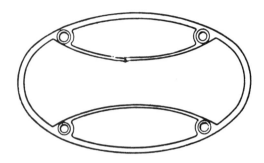

This specialized company claimed first use of
the trademark design shown here as October 9,
1925.

**Imperial Automobile Company,
Jackson, Michigan**

Imperial operated in the 1908-16 era, filing this
distinctive mark in January 1910. The company
claimed August 17, 1909, as the date of first use.

Indiana Truck Company, Marion, Indiana

1

Highway Freighters

2

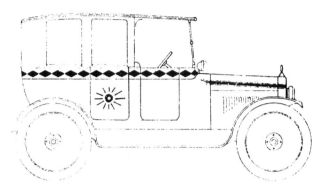

3

4

Left

Filed in June 1916 the Indiana mark shown at (1)
was first used January 1, 1912. Mark (2) was first
used in May 1918, and the Highway Freighters
mark (3) was first used in June 1920.

Mark (4) notes that "the portion with vertical lining indicates red. The portion with heavy
cross lining indicates black." This mark was first
used January 1, 1926.

**International Harvester Company,
Chicago, Illinois**

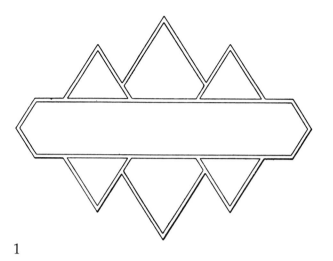

1

Prior to 1910, International Harvester was build-ing an "auto-buggy." In the 1920s the firm solid-ified its position in the motor truck industry. Mark (1) and mark (2) both claim first use as Oc-tober 1, 1924. Another well-known mark (3) is that of the Roadliner, first used November 15, 1949. The Loadstar mark (4) saw its first use on November 6 of that year. December 27, 1952, is noted as the first use of the Travelall mark (5).

Marks (6), (7), and (8) all refer to the heavy duty trucks and wagons, especially as used in various construction and manufacturing indus-tries. All claim a first use of April 18, 1955. The Scout mark (9) was first used January 1, 1958. However, mark (10) places the beginnings of the International truck line in perspective, noting a first use of 1907.

2

Roadliner

3

Loadstar

4

TRAVELALL

5

PAY

6

PAYWAGON

7

PAYHAULER

8

SCOUT

9

INTERNATIONAL

10

**International Motor Company,
New York, New York**

Mack

1

The Mack mark (1) shows a first use of October 13, 1911. Mark (2) for Year Round trucks was first used June 7, 1921. Mark (3), first used in September 1921, includes "Performance Counts" with Mark (1). Marks (4), (5), (6), and (7) all claim first use as September 21, 1921. Mark (8) was first used October 1, 1924, and the application notes that "no claim is made to the designation 'Great Coach' as historically used to describe the royal conveyance of the King of England." Mark (9) was first used December 16, 1930, and the mark (10) was first used November 1, 1932.

Year Round

2

3

PERFORMANCE COUNTS

BULL DOG

4

5

PERFORMANCE COUNTS

6

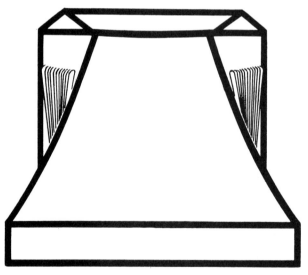

7

GREAT COACH

8

**International Motor Company,
New York, New York**

9

10

Alfred J. Jackson, Grand Rapids, Michigan

The Jacquet Flyer was one of those cars that saw a single completed copy and no more. The trademark, filed in December 1920, claims first use on November 5, 1919.

William H. Jahns, Los Angeles, California

Claiming use since January 10, 1916, the Tonford was essentially a conversion; the application states specifically, "truck attachments for converting passenger into freight-carrying automobiles."

Hugh S. Jarvis, New York, New York

HUJARVIS

Virtually nothing has been located in the course of this research concerning the HUJARVIS motor trucks. The company began using this mark on June 15, 1919.

Thomas B. Jeffery & Company, Kenosha, Wisconsin

1

2

The famous Quad motor truck was equipped with a trademark (1) claiming first use as September 1, 1913. Another mark (2) listed August 27, 1913, as the first use of this Jeffery mark as applied to automobiles.

Jordan Motor Car Company, Cleveland, Ohio

1

This company appears to have built cars in the 1917-31 period, with marks (1) and (2) being first used April 15, 1916. Mark (3) for the Silhouette tradename was first used on March 18, 1919, and the Line-Eight mark (4) was first used June 12, 1924. A Jordan 8 mark (5) was first used January 1, 1928, and the interesting Jordan mark (6) was first used May 1, 1929.

R. H. Jones & Company, New York, New York

Left
Of the various automotive histories consulted, nothing more than a confusing mass of Fulton operations have emerged, none of which seem to be related to the above firm. However, this Fulton mark was filed in September 1920, with the company claiming first use in March of that year.

Jordan Motor Car Company, Cleveland, Ohio

2

6

SILHOUETTE

3

LINE - EIGHT

4

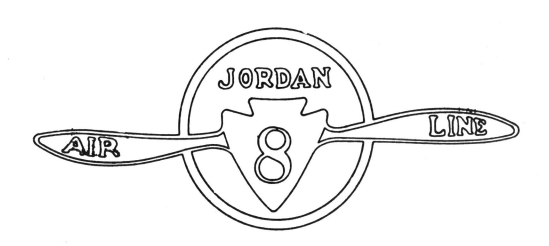

5

**Kaiser-Frazer Corporation,
Willow Run, Michigan**

1

2

Mark (1) for automobile engines was first used March 5, 1947; the company also noting that several other pertinent trademark registrations were in effect, namely, 435,365 and 435,364. Mark (2) for the interesting Henry J shows first use of May 10, 1950.

Julius Keller Jr., New York, New York

The Deemster was built at Hazleton, Pennsylvania in 1923. The parent company was Ogston Motor Company near London, England. This mark claims first use as February 1, 1923.

**Kelly-Springfield Motor Truck Company,
Springfield, Ohio**

1

KELLY

2

Both of the marks shown here were filed in October 1919. Mark (1) was first used May 1, 1913, and mark (2) was used first on March 1, 1914.

**Kenworth Motor Truck Corporation,
Seattle, Washington**

Kenworth filed for this trademark in April 1954, noting first use of October 1, 1944. The mark covered a wide range of equipment, included many kinds of trucks, service vehicles, motor tugs, trailers, and tank retrievers.

**Kentucky Wagon Mfg. Company,
Louisville, Kentucky**

Old Hickory gasoline trucks were an offshoot from a company who had been in the wagon and carriage business for many years. First use of this mark was made in February 1915 as applied to trucks; apparently the mark had been used for some years before as applied to wagons and other vehicles.

**Keystone Motor Company,
Philadelphia, Pennsylvania**

"Since April 15, 1900" was the claim to first use of this Autocycle mark from Keystone Motor Company. This was the only year that the Autocycle was built.

**Kissel Motor Car Company,
Hartford, Wisconsin**

1

Operating in the 1907-31 period, the first Kissel mark located for this project was (1), which claims first use of 1907. The KisselKar mark (2) was first used April 5, 1914.

**Kissel Motor Car Company,
Hartford, Wisconsin**

Kurtz Motor Car Company, Cleveland, Ohio

UNTEARABLE

Operating in the 1920-25 period, Kurtz filed this trademark in August 1924. The company claimed first use on May 5 of that year.

2

**Knickerbocker Motors Inc.,
New York, New York**

KNICKERBOCKER

Claiming use since April 1911, this mark from Knickerbocker was for motor-driven trucks.

**Knox Motor Truck Company,
Springfield, Massachusetts**

This fancy script-face Atlas trademark was filed by Knox on July 21, 1905. Virtually nothing further has appeared in the course of this project on Knox Motor Truck Company.

**La Fayette Motors Company,
Indianapolis, Indiana**

LA FAYETTE

Although La Fayette is generally considered to have operated in the 1921-24 period, this trademark application gives January 1, 1920, as the date of first use for the mark shown.

Fredrick A. La Roche, New York, New York

MULTIMOBILE.

In an application filed May 28, 1900, the Multimobile trademark was claimed as having first been used on September 15 of the previous year. No other information has been located.

**Laconia Truck Company,
Laconia, New Hampshire**

P · B · B

February 3, 1916, is when this P.B.B. trademark was first used; it was for motor trucks.

**Leach-Biltwell Motor Company,
Los Angeles, California**

This company built rather expensive cars in the 1920-23 period. The trademark shown here was first used in August 1919.

**H. T. Lathy Motor Company,
Cleveland Heights, Ohio**

Left
First used August 1, 1928, this mark "for automobiles" may or may not apply to a manufacturer; it is entirely possible that this firm might have been a dealer, or otherwise involved in the industry, since it does not appear in the various automotive histories consulted.

John Peter Lehrer, Belmont Park, New York

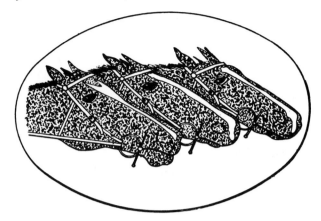

Automobile-vans and motor trucks were the items covered by this trademark, first used on March 16, 1921.

Irvin D. Leugel, Reading, Pennsylvania

This very fancy script artistry for the Meteor was typical of the period. First used January 17, 1902, the Meteor operation only operated for about two years.

Lexington Motor Company, Connersville, Indiana

1

2

The Lexington mark (1) was first used in 1916, but the application was not filed until 1921. Mark (2) was first used in June 1918. The company operated in the 1909-27 period.

Siegfried Leschziner, Newark, New Jersey

LESCINA

While actual production of the Lescina appears to have taken place in 1916, this mark claimed November 1, 1914, as the date of first use, and in fact, filed this application on November 6 of the following year.

**Liberty Motor Car Company,
Detroit, Michigan**

Liberty operated in the 1916-23 time frame, with this mark first being used in April 1916. Its description reads, "Consisting of the word 'Liberty' appearing upon a white background in the center of a shield design, the upper portion of the shield being in blue and the lower in red."

Lincoln Motor Company, Detroit, Michigan

1

Mark (1) for motor cars was first used in January 1931. Mark (2) for the Lincoln Zephyr was first used July 27, 1935. The latter mark also notes that the applicant owned registrations 317,334 and 213,146.

*Lincoln
Zephyr*

2

**Locomobile Company of America,
Bridgeport, Connecticut**

Locomobile

1

Locomobile

2

Locomobile began its career with a series of steam-powered vehicles in 1899 and ended life with numerous styles powered with gasoline engines.

The Locomobile mark at (1) was filed in 1905, and is only slightly different from mark (2) which claimed first use in June 1899. During 1899 and early 1900 came a virtual plethora of "Loco" trademarks, each denoting a specific type of vehicle. Mark (3) is for a Lococycle, while marks (4) through (17) are for various kinds of vehicles.

The Flint mark (18) was first used in October 1922 and was followed by two different JR-8 marks (19) and (20), both of which were first used in December 1924.

Lococycle

3

Locostage

4

Locotruck

5

Locomail

6

**Locomobile Company of America,
Bridgeport, Connecticut**

Locolaunch

7

Locowagon

8

Lococab

9

Locohack

10

Loco

11

Locobus

12

Locotrap

13

Locolene

14

**Locomobile Company of America,
Bridgeport, Connecticut**

Lococar

15

Locoracer

16

Locodelivery

17

18

JR-8

19

**Locomobile Company of America,
Bridgeport, Connecticut**

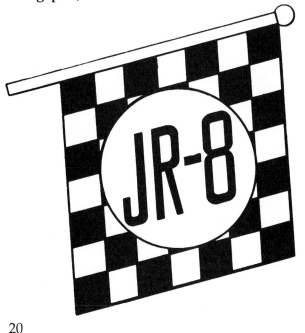

20

**Los Angeles Creamery Company,
Los Angeles, California**

Motor trucks were the source of trade for this Electruck trademark. Used since June 15, 1912, the mark was not filed until October 1924.

**Louisiana Motor Car Company,
Shreveport, Louisiana**

Originally at Detroit (1916-17), then in Indiana (1918), and finally to Louisiana in the 1919-22 period, the Bour-Davis was registered with this trademark in 1920; it claimed first use in October of 1918.

Geneva B. Lodge, Detroit, Michigan

Operating in the 1910-11 period, the DeMot trademark shown here was filed in December 1909. Little is known of this company.

**Lovejoy Manufacturing Company,
Boston, Massachusetts**

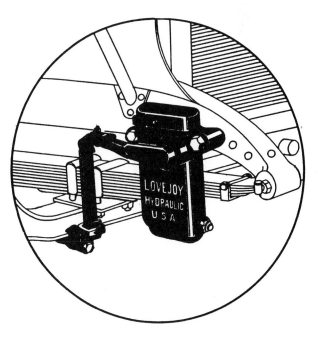

During 1920 and 1921 the Lorraine car was built, according to the various automotive histories. However, the *Patent Office Gazette* carrying this application shows October 22, 1918, to be the date of first use.

1

**Lovejoy Manufacturing Company,
Boston, Massachusetts**

2

Although the Lovejoy shock absorbers certainly have nothing to do with automotive manufacturers *per se,* these two interesting marks seemed worthy of inclusion. Mark (1) was first used in August 1919 and mark (2) was first used August 21, 1922.

John Luntz, Jr., Baltimore, Maryland

Lord Baltimore

Organized in 1910, the Lord Baltimore Motor Car Company manufactured trucks and, in 1913 only, built a motor car. Their Lord Baltimore trademark indicates a first use of January 26, 1910.

**McFarlan Motor Company,
Connersville, Indiana**

William H. McIntyre, Auburn, Indiana

The Imp trademark was for a cycle car and was first used September 2, 1913. Automotive historians generally note that the company operated in the 1913-14 period.

**McIntosh Hardware Corporation,
Cleveland, Ohio**

HERCULES

This particular Hercules model does not appear in the automotive histories consulted, although there are numerous other manufacturers who applied the Hercules tradename to cars. This mark was for "bicycles and automobiles" and was filed in December 1906.

Left
Operating in the 1910-28 period, McFarlan adopted this trademark design in 1913, claiming September 27 of that year as the date of first use. Application to register this mark was not made however, until February 1919.

**Maccar Truck Company,
Scranton, Pennsylvania**

December 10, 1912, was the date that this mark was first applied to Maccar trucks. No other information has surfaced on this company.

Maibohm Motors Company, Sandusky, Ohio

In the car business from 1916 to 1922, Maibohm had begun already in 1886 as a wagon and carriage builder. This mark, first used in 1916, was filed in October 1920.

**Malcolm Motor Car Company of New York,
New York, New York**

This mark was first used March 15, 1915. We have been unable to determine if this was the same firm as operated at Detroit, Michigan, about the same time.

**Marmon Motor Car Company,
Indianapolis, Indiana**

1

Marmon began building cars already in 1902, with the company remaining in business until 1933. After this the Marmon-Herrington Company was formed to build trucks; the latter remained into the 1960s.

Mark (1) is for the Roosevelt 8, with first use being January 9, 1929. Mark (2) is a different form of the Roosevelt 8 trademark; it too claims first use in January 1929.

Mark (3) for Marmon-Herrington trucks was first used June 30, 1931, and the Marmon-Herrington All Wheel Drive mark (4) was first used October 30, 1935.

**Marmon Motor Car Company,
Indianapolis, Indiana**

2

3

4

**Marco Mfg. Company,
Wheatland, Pennsylvania**

MARCO

No information has been located on the Marco
except that it was "for motorized four-wheel vehicles for personnel and equipment." It was first
used October 31, 1953.

Marquette Company, Detroit, Michigan

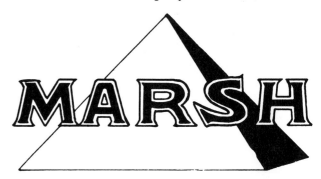

This mark was for "automobiles and motor
trucks" and was filed April 9, 1912. The company claimed first use in December of the previous
year.

Marsh Motor Car Company, Cleveland, Ohio

MARSH

Marsh operated in the 1920-23 period and
claimed first use of this mark to be December
26, 1919.

Mason Motor Truck Company, Flint, Michigan

RoadKing

The Road King trademark from Mason was first used March 31, 1922. We have no further information on this company.

W. N. Matthews Corporation, St. Louis, Missouri

This mark from January 1923 is "for motor and hand propelled trucks." Aside from this application of October 1927, we have no further data on the company.

Maxwell Motor Company, Detroit, Michigan

1

Prior to 1913, Maxwell operated at various locations, but in the 1913-25 period, the company settled in Detroit. Mark (1), filed in 1913, notes a first use of August 15, 1908. Mark (2) gives the same date for first use, but was filed in 1920. Used since 1914, mark (3) was also filed in 1920; mark (4) was first used September 7, 1921, and was filed the following year

Maxfer Truck Company, Chicago, Illinois

MAXFER·TON·TRUCK·MAKER

The particular description of the "Maxfer-Ton-Truck-Maker" mark includes "automobile trucks and units and . . . parts thereof." Having no additional information on this company, the description naturally leads to the assumption that this was a conversion unit for making a truck out of a car.

Maxwell Motor Company, Detroit, Michigan

2

MAXWELL

3

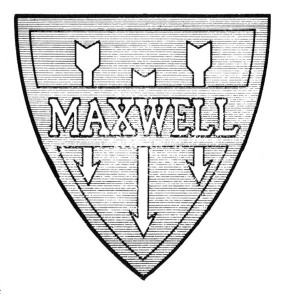

4

Meccas Mfg. & Specialty Company, New York, New York

MECCA 400

Automotive historians usually give 1915 and 1916 as the production years for the Mecca; however, this Mecca 400 mark lists April 1912 as the date of first use, with a filing date of April 14, 1915.

Menominee Motor Truck Company, Clintonville, Wisconsin

The Hurryton mark was first used on March 1, 1920, and was filed in November 1922. Little other information has surfaced on this company.

**Mercer Automobile Company,
Trenton, New Jersey**

The Mercer line was built from 1910 to 1926, with this mark claiming first use in December 1910. It was filed in October 1918.

**Metallurgique Motor Company,
New York, New York**

Actually a product of Belgium, this make was built in the 1898-1928 period. The mark shown here was first used on January 7, 1911.

Midland Motor Company, Moline, Illinois

**Millspaugh & Irish Corporation,
Indianapolis, Indiana**

Not an automobile builder, this firm specialized in building automobile bodies. The Shamrock mark shown here was first used on May 27, 1925.

**Minerva Motors, Berchem, near Antwerp,
Belgium**

Minerva filed this mark on June 27, 1910. The company claimed first use of the mark in 1897, and continued in the automobile business until 1939.

Left
This firm was a successor to the Deere-Clarke motor car; Midland functioned from 1908 to 1913. The Midland mark shown here was first used in July 1908.

Minneapolis Steel & Machinery Company, Minneapolis, Minnesota

The Twin City line from Minneapolis Steel had made a big name for itself in the tractor business some years prior to the May 20, 1919, first usage of the term as applied to motor trucks.

Mitchell-Lewis Motor Company, Racine, Wisconsin

This firm was in the automobile business for twenty years, beginning in 1903. However, they had been building carriages for some years before, thus this mark claims first use of January 1, 1885.

Moline Plow Company, Moline, Illinois

Monarch

Organized in 1913, the company claimed this mark to have been first used on May 15. Monarch remained in business until 1916.

Moon Motor Car Company, St. Louis, Missouri

Although the company operated in the 1905-29 period, this mark was not adopted until September 27, 1915.

Moreland Motor Truck Company, Los Angeles, California

Little information has surfaced on Moreland, except for this trademark, first used July 31, 1911.

Left
Moline Plow Company was a long-time farm machinery manufacturer, but the Stephens automobile trademark was first used in 1916. The claim was filed in September 1920.

Morris Adler Company, Quincy, Illinois

No information has been located on this company outside of the mark shown here; it was first used January 1, 1915.

Motor Car Manufacturing Company, Indianapolis, Indiana

Operating in the 1912-17 period, this company first used the Pathfinder mark shown here on August 1, 1911.

Motor World Publishing Company, New York, New York

Numerous automobile magazines became available, their numbers paralleling the organization of many new manufacturers. One example is Motor World, a publication which filed this mark in October 1916. This one was found simply by chance, as our research was not aimed toward searching out publishing companies. It is included simply as a reminder that the automotive press was highly involved and was very influential in molding the emerging automotive industries.

Mototeria Company, Cleveland, Ohio

Traveling grocers were fairly popular, especially in areas where grocery stores were at a distance. One firm specializing in vehicles, primarily trucks, used in this work was the Mototeria; it claimed first use of this mark on July 1, 1923.

Andrew Murphy & Son, Omaha, Nebraska

No information has surfaced concerning this company, except for the mark shown. It was first used January 1, 1907, and was filed in December 1911.

Walter M. Murphy Motors Company, Los Angeles, California

This company specialized in "automobile coaches and bodies and steam car coaches and bodies." The mark shown here was first used September 21, 1925.

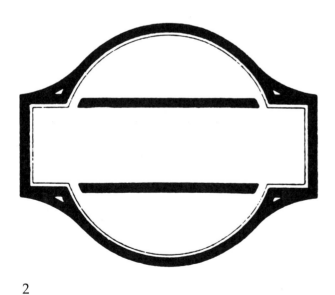

1

Nash built cars from 1917 to 1942. Mark (1) notes that it was first used on April 2, 1917, as was mark (2). Filed on May 16, 1928, mark (3) was first used just six days earlier. The LaFayette mark (4) is a portrait of Marquis de Lafayette; it was first used January 6, 1934. Marks (5) and (6) were both filed by the Nash-Kelvinator Corporation on May 22, 1950. The Rambler mark (5) was first used on August 1, 1900, and the Statesman mark (6) was first used September 22, 1949.

3

2

4

Nash Motors Company, Kenosha, Wisconsin

Rambler

5

Statesman

6

National Motor Vehicle Company, Indianapolis, Indiana

National built numerous models during its 1900-1924 existence. This fancy script mark was first used in November 1905, although it was not filed until June 1914.

Nelson Bros. Company, Saginaw, Michigan

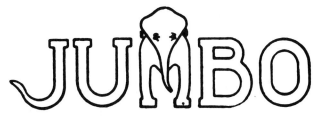

Jumbo trucks gained a wide reputation, with this mark being first used April 1, 1916.

New Merlin Cycle Company, Birmingham, England

AUTOCRAT

New York Motor Vehicle Company, New York, New York

VOLOMOBILE

From various historical sources it is believed that a very few Volomobiles were built during 1902. The company claimed first use of this mark in June 1900. The application notes the essential feature of the mark, namely, "the word 'VOLOMOBILE' beneath the representation of a motor carriage, to which a pair of outstretched wings is attached at the forward traverse spring, and the representation of clouds supporting the motor carriage."

Left
It is curious that the Autocrat mark should have been filed in the U.S. at this early period since it was built in England; the company claimed first use of the mark on February 6, 1919. Perhaps some of the Autocrats made their way into the U.S. about that time.

New York Transportation Company, New York, New York

This mark was for "motor buses and parts thereof" and was first used in May 1920; the company filed the application in August

Nordyke & Marmon Company, Indianapolis, Indiana

Nordyke & Marmon are better known in many circles as manufacturers of flour milling machinery, although the company was in the automobile business from 1902 to 1933. This Marmon mark was first used in early 1903 and was filed in July 1917.

Oakland Motor Car Co. of Michigan, Pontiac, Michigan

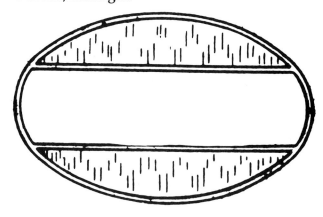

Oakland operated from 1907 to 1931, after which time it became Pontiac. This mark was first used in February 1916.

William Scott O'Connor, New York, New York

Rotamobile.

The Rotamobile does not appear in any of the historical references we have searched, probably because production was very limited, or perhaps it never began at all. This mark was first used January 10, 1900.

Oklahoma Auto Mfg. Company, North Muskogee, Oklahoma

First used in September 1917, this mark was for motor trucks and trailers.

110

**Olds Motor Works,
Detroit and Lansing, Michigan**

OLDSMOBILE

1

Although Olds Motor Vehicle Company was established already in 1897, this "Oldsmobile" mark claimed first use in December 1900 (1), (2). In 1942 the company title changed to the Oldsmobile Division of General Motors.

OLDSMOBILE

2

**Oneida Motor Truck Company,
Green Bay, Wisconsin**

1

No information has been located thus far to indicate when Oneida began building trucks, but mark (1) was first used June 1, 1917. The description notes, "a circular band, a horizontal bar superimposed upon the band, said band and bar being black, the word 'Oneida' in red upon the bar, and an Indian and canoe below the bar. . . ." Mark (2) for Uncommon Carriers was first used December 1, 1918.

UNCOMMON CARRIERS

2

**Oshkosh Motor Truck Company,
Oshkosh, Wisconsin**

OSHKOSH 4-WHEEL-DRIVE

This mark for the Oshkosh 4-Wheel-Drive was first used New Year's Day, 1919.

Overman Automobile Company, Chicopee, Massachusetts

VICTOR

Overman appears to have been active in the 1899-1903 period, building steam automobiles primarily. The Victor mark shown here was first used May 1, 1900, and was filed May 18, 1901.

Overseas Products Corporation, New York, New York

VICTORY

No information has been located on the Victory motor trucks and automobiles; the company notes first use of the mark as January 2, 1919.

Owen Magnetic Car Company, Philadelphia, Pennsylvania

The Owen Magnetic appears at various geographical locations in the 1915-21 period, with the mark shown here being first used October 1, 1916.

Packard Motor Car Company, Detroit, Michigan

1

Packard began life in 1899, became Studebaker-Packard in 1955, and ended its life in 1958. Mark (1) illustrates the heavy script mark used for many years. Marks (2) and (3) covered various lubricants sold under the Packard name; both of these marks were filed in 1908. June 6, 1910, was the first use of marks (4), (5), and (6). Marks (4) and (5) were filed in 1910; mark (6) was not filed until January 1934.

2

3

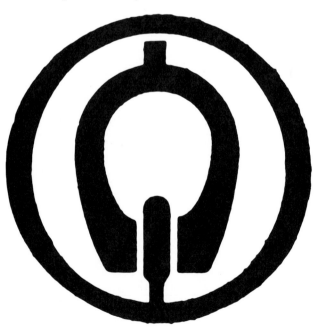

**Packard Motor Car Company,
Detroit, Michigan**

4

5

6

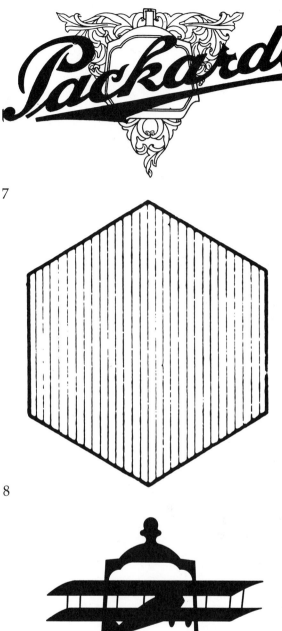

7

8

9

The rather impressive mark shown at (7) was first used May 10, 1911. First use of the red hexagonal figure (8) was given as January 1, 1913. In 1919 Packard made first use of mark (9) with the representation of an aeroplane upon the outline of a radiator. Mark (10) was filed on February 6, 1941, with reference being made to Trademark No. 47,621 of November 14, 1905, and renewed. This particular mark covered internal combustion engines and their parts, structural parts, and accessories.

**Packard Motor Car Company,
Detroit, Michigan**

Packard

10

ASK
THE MAN
WHO OWNS
ONE

11

12

13

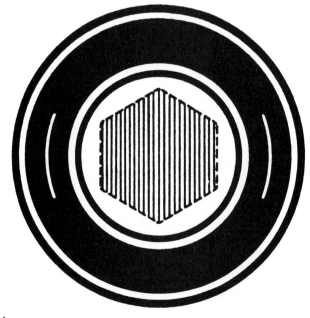

14

"Ask the Man Who Owns One" was a trademark (11) first used by Packard in 1923. In October 1925 the company first used mark (12) for its automobiles. Although it was not filed until 1951, the company claimed first use of their "A Blue Ribbon Car" mark (13) in 1936, applying it to "motor cars and trucks." Mark (14) was first used "as early as 1936." It consisted of a series of concentric black circles with the central hexagon in red, which "when rotating appears to be circular."

**Packard Motor Car Company,
Detroit, Michigan**

Clipper

15

MAYFAIR

16

SPORTSTER

17

CAVALIER

18

BOCA RATON

19

PALM BEACH

20

21

EXECUTIVE

22

PANTHER

23

24

The Clipper mark (15) was first used May 23, 1941, although not filed until August 1952. The Mayfair mark (16) was first used in January 1951. Then came the Sportster mark (17) in October 1952, followed by the Cavalier mark (18) in November of that year. In 1953, April to be exact, Packard made first use of their Boca Raton mark (19), with the Palm Beach mark (20) being initiated the same time. The interesting ship's wheel (21) with a hexagon in the center was first used between October 15 and November 30, 1953. The Panama mark (22) was actually filed by Studebaker-Packard, naming December 1, 1953, as the date of first use. This mark was filed in February 1954. The same holds true for the Panther mark (23) used since January 28, 1954, and the Executive mark (24) first used in April 1955.

**Paige-Detroit Motor Car Company,
Detroit, Michigan**

Paige operated in the 1909-28 period. The mark shown here was first used in 1914, although it was not filed until October 1918.

Palace Cab Company, New York, New York

No information has been located on this company, outside of the mark shown here; it claimed first use in October 1931.

Palmer & Singer Mfg. Company, New York, New York

1

No information has come to our attention regarding the Palmer & Singer operation, except for marks (1) and (2), both claiming first use on November 15, 1913, and filed the following month.

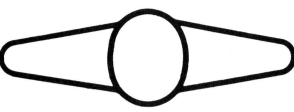

2

Pan American Motor Company, Mamaroneck, New York

PANAM

This company first adopted the tradename "PANAM" on June 1, 1901. Operations apparently ran during 1902 and 1903.

Samuel C. Pandolfo, St. Cloud, Minnesota

1

While automotive historians usually indicate a production period of 1919-21 for the PAN Motor Company cars, mark (1) claims a first use of September 14, 1916, and a filing date of November 1917. Mark (2) was first used January 1, 1918, and filed September 29 of the following year.

Samuel C. Pandolfo, St. Cloud, Minnesota

2

Bennett J. Patrick, Minneapolis, Minnesota

This mark, first used June 20, 1918, was apparently applied to tractors, as well as motor trucks.

**Paramount Taxicab Corporation,
New York, New York**

Our research has failed to disclose whether the Luxor from Paramount was related to the Luxor automobiles built earlier at Hagerstown, Maryland. The mark shown here claimed first use of May 22, 1932.

Clarke D. Pease, Inc., New York, New York

No information aside from this mark has been located on this firm. The mark, first used in October 1923, consisted of "the letters 'H. S.' within a circle. . . ."

**Parker Motor Truck Company,
Milwaukee, Wisconsin**

Parker filed this mark in August 1919, having first used it only one month previously.

Peerless Motor Car Company, Cleveland, Ohio

Peerless operated in the 1900-31 period. This Peerless Six mark was "used since March 6, 1924."

Pierce-Arrow Motor Car Company, Buffalo, New York

1

2

Pierce-Arrow operated in the 1901-38 time frame. Mark (1) was for automobiles and motor trucks, and was first used in 1901. Marks (2) and (3) likewise saw their first use in 1901. Mark (4) was for axles; this mark had been in use for automobiles and trucks since 1901 and was first used on axles in 1918. Frames for automobiles were covered in mark (5), with 1901 being claimed as the first use. Mark (6) was for pedal pads, and 1903 was the first use in this regard; mark (7) for "foot mats of rubber products and fabrics" was first used in 1903. Yet another arrow mark (8) saw first use in 1903, although the application for this mark was not filed until 1925.

3

4

5

6

7

8

9

The chassis was protected with this trademark application (9) of 1923, but first used in 1903. In 1927 came a distinctive mark (10) for "automobiles, trucks, buses, taxicabs, and their component parts." It was first used on April 8 of that year. Another style, the Fleet Arrow mark (11) was first used in February 1928, as was the Pierce mark (12) and another Fleet Arrow design (13). Yet another Pierce-Arrow design (14) made its first appearance on January 21, 1931.

**Pierce-Arrow Motor Car Company,
Buffalo, New York**

10

=FLEET ARROW=

11

PIERCE

12

FLEET ARROW

13

PIERCE ARROW

14

James H. Pierce, Bay City, Michigan

The Winner truck trademark shown here was
first used March 12, 1920.

**Pilgrim Motor Car Company,
Detroit, Michigan**

First used January 13, 1915, this Pilgrim mark is
the only one we located for this company, which
operated in the 1915-18 period.

Pilot Motor Car Company, Richmond, Indiana

Various models of Pilot cars were built between
1909 and 1924. This mark claims first use on
May 1, 1910.

**Playboy Motor Car Corporation,
Buffalo, New York**

1

The Playboy marks (1) and (2) were applied for
in November 1947, claiming first use on February 18 of that year.

2

**Pope Manufacturing Company,
Hartford, Connecticut**

1

The Columbia mark (1) and the circular mark
(2) were both filed in 1905, the mark (3) being
filed in January 1907. The company began operations in 1904, continuing thus for a decade.

2

3

Premier Motors, Inc., Indianapolis, Indiana

1

Premier Motors, Inc., Indianapolis, Indiana

2

4

The Premier mark (1) was filed in November 1905 as was "The Quality Car" mark at (2). Another Premier mark (3), filed in 1917, notes a first use of January 1, 1903. Passenger Automobiles and Taxicabs were included in the application shown at (4); it claimed first use of August 1, 1915. Mark (5) was claimed as having a first use of February 16, 1925, noting that "the Indian Head however, has been continuously used in association with the word Premier since about June or July 1923." Premier operated in the 1902-26 period. Another Premier mark (6) filed in 1925 included taxicabs, delivery trucks, and commercial vehicles, as well as automobiles.

3

5

6

R. C. H. Corporation, Detroit, Michigan

This Detroit firm listed August 1, 1911 as first use of the mark shown here; its manufacturing activities ran from 1912 to 1915.

Rainier Motor Corporation, Flushing, New York

1

Mark (1) for this company was filed in April 1906 for automobiles. Mark (2), filed in 1919, claimed usage since 1906, but for motor trucks. This company operated at Flushing until 1907, then moved to Saginaw, Michigan, operating there until 1911, and finally was acquired by General Motors.

2

Ralston Iron Works, San Francisco, California

Ralston built an attachment for converting pleasure cars into motor trucks. It claimed first use of this mark on January 11, 1916.

Reliance Motor Truck Company, Appleton, Wisconsin

Filed in March 1920, Reliance claimed first use of this mark on December 15, 1911.

Remington Motors Inc., New York, New York

Between 1895 and 1904 Remington Arms Company at Ilion, New York, had attempted the automobile business. Whether the mark shown here was in any way connected to the famous arms manufacturer has yet to be made manifest, since this mark claims a first use of 1916.

Reo Motor Car Company, Lansing, Michigan

1

2

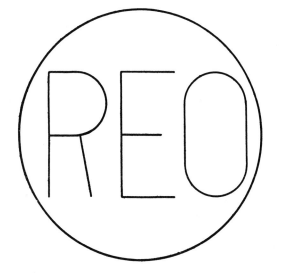

3

Reo operated in a 1905-36 time frame, with mark (1) being filed in 1906 under the title of Reo Car Company. The Speed Wagon mark (2) was first used May 3, 1919, and an elaborate Speed Wagon mark (3) was first used July 1, 1922. The Heavy Duty Speed Wagon mark (4) saw first use June 1, 1925. The rather plain Reo mark (5) was first used in October 1925 and applied to "constructive parts for automobiles." Mark (6) used the letters "R I O"; this mark, first used in December 1925, was for automobiles. Mark (7) for the Wolverine saw first use on February 10, 1926, and November 10 of that year was the first use of the Flying Cloud trademark (8). At (9) is yet another Reo mark; it was first used February 27, 1934.

4

5

Reo Motor Car Company, Lansing, Michigan

6

9

7

8

Republic Motor Truck Company, Alma, Michigan

1

FLEETMASTER

2

Mark (1) for the Republic trucks was first used July 5, 1921, with mark (2) for the Fleetmaster seeing first use on April 22, 1929.

**Revere Motor Car Corporation,
Logansport, Indiana**

1

Three different marks have been located for Revere. Mark (1) notes that "the mark is shown with the word 'Revere' above a horse and rider in silver color. The surrounding ring is blue and the side panels red." Mark (2) indicates a blue circle surrounding a gold-colored field. All three marks claim first use on January 1, 1917.

2

3

**Rickenbacker Motor Company,
Detroit, Michigan**

1

Mark (1) was first used in July 1921, while mark (2) was first used December 1, 1925. This company operated in the 1922-27 period.

2

**Rockford Automobile & Engine Company,
Rockford, Illinois**

This mark was filed April 11, 1908. Little else has been found on this firm.

Rockne Motors Corporation, Detroit, Michigan

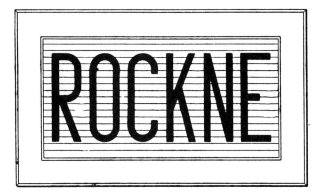

1

This company operated during 1932 and 1933. Mark (1) was first used May 28, 1931, followed by mark (2), first used February 22, 1932.

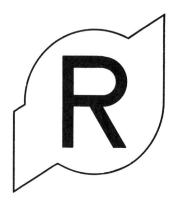

2

Rollin Motors Company, Euclid, Ohio

1

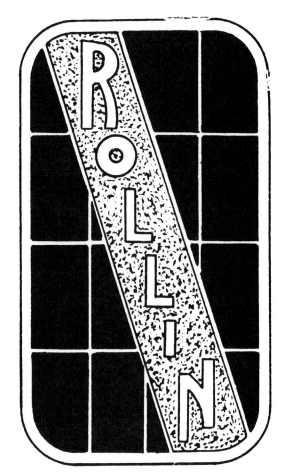

2

Royal Martel Corporation, New York, New York

This mark was for motor vehicles, but for taxi-cabs in particular. It was first used May 24, 1925.

The Rubay Company, Cleveland, Ohio

Leon Rubay built a line of automobiles during 1922 and 1923. This mark was first used December 22, 1921.

St. Louis Motor Carriage Company, St. Louis, Missouri

The Saint Louis

Production of this vehicle appears to have run from 1899 to 1905, although this mark, filed in 1905, claims to have been in use for ten years.

Samson Tractor Company, Janesville, Wisconsin

GENEMO

The Genemo mark was for "automobiles, motor trucks, motor lorries, and motor cars." It claimed first use in September 1920.

Sanford Motor Truck Company, Syracuse, New York

This mark, filed in June 1920, claimed first use in June 1910.

Sandow Motor Truck Company, Chicago, Illinois

SANDOW

Filed May 24, 1920, this mark for the Sandow trucks shows a first use date of early 1912.

Saxon Motor Company, Detroit, Michigan

SAXON

Operating in the 1913-22 era, this Saxon trademark was first used March 1, 1914.

**Augustus T. Schlater,
Philadelphia, Pennsylvania**

No information has been located on the Samobile. The mark was filed in April 1913, with first use being claimed for the previous February.

William E. Schneider, Washington, D.C.

Autocarette

This venture operated during 1900 and 1901, with the application claiming January 20, 1900, as first use of the Autocarette mark.

Scripps-Booth Company, Detroit, Michigan

**Searchmont Motor Company,
Philadelphia, Pennsylvania**

SEARCHMONT

Operating only in the 1900-03 period, Searchmont first used this trademark October 15, 1900.

**Selden Motor Vehicle Company,
Rochester, New York**

1

Selden began building automobiles in 1907, continuing until 1914. Motor trucks then occupied the company until 1932. Mark (1) is for the Selden automobile. This mark was filed in May 1909. The Roadmaster mark (2) was first used in April 1925.

ROADMASTER

2

Left
This company began business in 1912, continuing for a decade. The mark shown here was first used in August 1914.

J. M. Selzer Carriage & Business Wagon Mfg. Co., St. Louis, Missouri

This company was not an automobile builder, but built automobile bodies in addition to its wagons and carriages. This mark was first used in December 1912.

Service Motor Truck Company, Wabash, Indiana

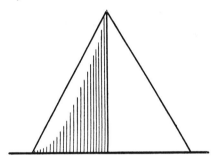

1

2

Service filed four different marks in 1920. Mark (1), first used August 21, is a simple pyramid. Mark (2), of October, is a figure of a pyramid, plus the word; mark (3) is a pyramid within a circle, and the word "Service." Mark (4), of September 15, 1920, is for the Red Pyramid motor trucks.

3

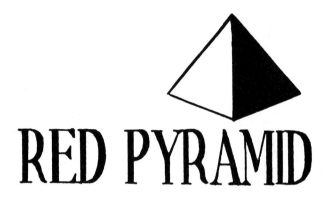

4

Seven-Eleven Auto Company, New Orleans, Louisiana

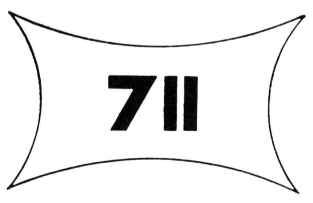

No information can be located on the 711 mark shown here except that it was filed in March 1920 and claimed first use on January 16, 1916.

**Sheridan Commercial Car Company,
Chicago, Illinois**

Automobiles and motor trucks were both
named as products of this firm. Their claim was
to January 17, 1916, as first use of the mark

**Sheridan Motor Car Company,
Muncie, Indiana**

Sheridan operated only during 1920 and 1921.
Their mark claimed first use on April 15, 1920.

**Signal Motor Truck Company,
Detroit, Michigan**

This Signal mark for motor trucks was first used
in March 1913.

**Simplex Automobile Company,
New York, New York**

In all, Simplex operated from 1907 to 1919. This
mark, filed in 1920, shows first use of January
1913.

**Skelton Motors Corporation,
St. Louis, Missouri**

Only from 1920-1922 did this company build
cars. Their trademark application indicates February 1, 1920, as the date of first use for this
mark.

Standard Motor Truck Company, Detroit, Michigan

This mark from Standard indicates that it was first used in August 1912.

John Stanley Small, Detroit, Michigan

CAVAC (arranged as a cross)

The CAVAC was built only during 1910 and 1911, with this mark showing a first use of April 1910.

Smith Form-A-Truck Company, Seattle, Washington

Form-a-Truck

First used in March 1915, this trademark referred to a conversion attachment whereby an automobile could be converted into a truck or delivery vehicle.

Charles Albert Smith, Windsor, Ontario, Canada

TONSMORE

The Tonsmore mark shown here referred to "automobile-trucks," possibly to a conversion unit for making a truck out of a car. This mark was first used June 1, 1917.

Snowmobile Company, West Ossippee, New Hampshire

SNOWMOBILE

The Snowmobile mark shown here was first used September 18, 1923. It was for "land motor vehicles . . ., said vehicles including tanks . . ." Products included a conversion unit whereby a truck could be converted into a "Snowmobile."

Southern Motor Mfg. Association, Houston, Texas

The Southern mark shown here was first used April 7, 1920. This firm also sold farm tractors, as well as automobiles and motor trucks.

Speedwell Motor Car Company, Dayton, Ohio

SPEEDWELL

Speedwell built cars in the 1907-14 period. This mark, filed in December 1907, indicated that it had been used for ten years. However, the application was specifically for "carriages, carts, buggies, and wagons." Whether this mark was ever used in connection with Speedwell automobiles is presently unknown.

**Stability Motors Company,
Philadelphia, Pennsylvania**

Stability specialized in motor trucks, with this mark first being used on January 11, 1918.

**Standard Motor Truck Company,
Detroit, Michigan**

Although it was not filed until August 1924, this mark claimed first use already in March 1893. Included in the description were horse and motor vehicles, trucks, chassis, and bodies.

**Standard Steel Car Company,
Pittsburgh, Pennsylvania**

1

Mark (1) was for automobiles, with Standard claiming first use on November 3, 1913. Mark (2) included automobiles and motor trucks, with a first use of January 19, 1915.

2

**Star Motors Incorporated,
New York, New York**

1

Star was in the automobile business during the 1922-28 period. The Star mark shown at (1) consisted of "a white enamel star outlined in silver on a black enameled field surrounded by a white enamel ring bordered with silver rings." This mark was first used in May 1922. Mark (2) for the Rugby was first used in September 1923; the Rugby was an export version of the Star.

**Star Motors Incorporated,
New York, New York**

2

Stephens Motor Car Company, Moline, Illinois

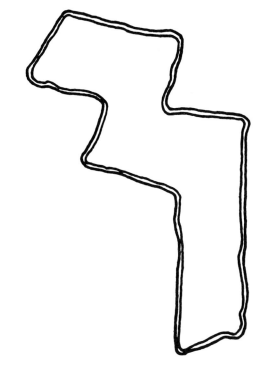

1

Operating in the 1917-24 time frame, the company filed marks (1) and (2) in February 1923, claiming first use as of December 1, 1922.

F. B. Stearns Company, Cleveland, Ohio

Up to 1911 this company built the Stearns automobiles, and from 1912 to 1929 built the Stearns-Knight. This mark, filed in May 1927, claimed first use in November 1922.

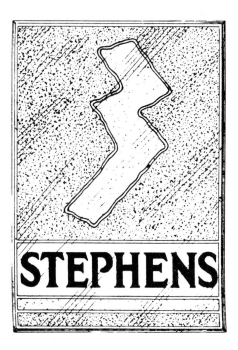

2

J. G. Sterling, Warren, Ohio

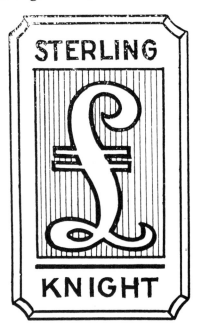

First at Cleveland, and then at Warren, Ohio, this company built cars from 1920 to 1926. The mark shown here claimed first use in May of 1921.

Sterling Motor Truck Company, Milwaukee, Wisconsin

1

RED-HEAD

2

The Sterling mark at (1) was first used February 29, 1916; it, like the others shown here, related to this specific enterprise. Mark (2) was filed in September 1927, and Mark (3) noted a first use of November 5, 1914; the latter mark was filed in August 1947.

3

Vincent G. Apple, Dayton, Ohio

STEELMOBILE

The Steelmobile mark claimed first use in October 1903. Vincent G. Apple went on to develop numerous ignition devices.

Stevens-Duryea Inc., Chicopee, Massachusetts

This company endured in the automobile business from 1901 to 1927. The mark shown here was filed in January 1921, although the company claimed first use on January 1, 1910.

Stewart Motor Company, Buffalo, New York

This firm, specializing in motor trucks, built an automobile during 1915 and 1916. The mark shown here had a claimed first use date of June 1913.

Harold G. Stiles, Chicago, Illinois

The Tonhustler appears to have been a conversion unit for making a truck out of a car. The mark shown here was first used November 28, 1922.

Melvin Stringer, Pottstown, Pennsylvania

The Mel Special was built in the 1918-24 period, with this mark first being used September 15, 1924.

Studebaker Corporation, South Bend, Indiana

1

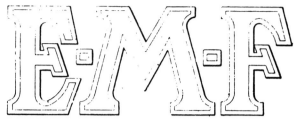

2

Studebaker had a long history as a wagon and carriage maker, with mark (1) going back to 1867. Mark (2) was filed in 1911 and was first used September 1, 1908. Automobile tires were the subject of the mark shown at (3), with May 3, 1919, being the date of first use. At (4) is shown the mark for "automobile bodies" first used in September 1924.

3

4

The impressive mark at (5) for The President was first used on June 25, 1926. Also in 1926 came the ATALANTA (6); it was first used on July 7. Mark (7) for The Little Aristocrat was first used in August 1926, and mark (8) for the Chancellor had a first use of July 12. Another mark first used on that date was the Commander, shown at (9). Another version of the Commander mark is shown at (10); it was first used July 13, 1927.

5

ATALANTA

6

THE LITTLE ARISTOCRAT

7

CHANCELLOR

8

COMMANDER

9

THE COMMANDER

10

The Cadet mark at (11) was first used in March 1927, followed by two versions of The Director. Mark (12) was first used on July 5, and Mark (13) was first used July 21, 1927. Mark (14) refers to internal combustion engines, and Mark (15) was for automobiles. Both were first used in April 1927. The Erskine mark (16) came into being August 2, 1928, with the Richelieu mark (17) following the next month.

THE CADET

11

DIRECTOR

12

THE DIRECTOR

13

14

15

Studebaker Corporation, South Bend, Indiana

16

RICHELIEU

17

Commander

18

ZEPHYR

19

20

Passmaster

21

VICTORY SIX

22

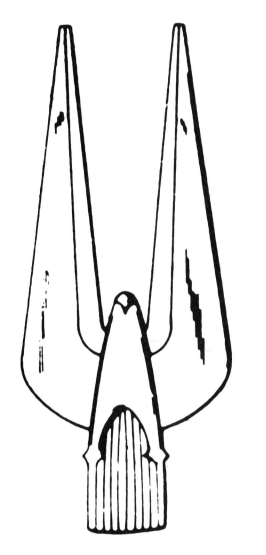

23

On December 20, 1935, Studebaker first used the Commander mark (18), and the Zephyr mark (19) was first used in September of that year. Mark (20) came on September 15, 1950, while marks (21) and (22) were first used December 27, 1954. Mark (23) saw first use in August 1956.

Including various mergers, Studebaker built cars and trucks from 1902 to 1966.

**Stutz Motor Car Company,
Indianapolis, Indiana**

1

The Stutz was built from 1911 to 1935. Mark (1)
was first used December 10, 1925, and was an
elaborate design of blue, orange, green, and
black. The Stutz mark (2) followed with first use
on December 15, 1927, and mark (3) was first
used December 29, 1928.

2

3

S. Sumner Shears, New York, New York

First used on June 20, 1915, this mark was for
the Du Pont automobiles.

**E. R. Thomas Motor Company,
Buffalo, New York**

Thomas built cars from 1903 to 1918; in fact, the
Author's grandfather bought one in 1909.
Thomas filed this trademark in April 1910.

George L. Thompson, New York, New York

The Banker's Express mark shown here was first used on August 10, 1916; it was filed a month later.

Toledo Carriage Woodwork Company, Toledo, Ohio

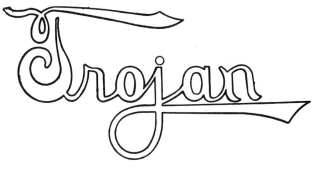

No information whatever has been located on this Trojan automobile mark, first used November 21, 1912, and filed in February 1913.

The Touraine Company, Philadelphia, Pennsylvania

H. M. Tower Corporation, West Haven, Connecticut

ROAD HOUND

Road Hound motor trucks first took the mark shown here on March 23, 1923.

Traffic Motor Truck Corporation, St. Louis, Missouri

1

Mark (1) is a mark for Traffic motor trucks first used on July 7, 1917; mark (2) was first used October 27, 1921, on the Speedboy trucks.

Speedboy

2

Left
This company appears to have been active in the 1913-14 period, with the mark shown here claiming first use on December 5, 1913.

**Transport Truck Company,
Mount Pleasant, Michigan**

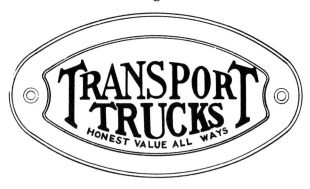

November 3, 1919, is the date of first use for this decorative mark from Transport Truck Company.

**Mitten Traylor Inc.,
Philadelphia, Pennsylvania**

AUTOMOTRAM

The Automotram mark shown here was first used April 14, 1923. It applied to "self-propelled vehicles, single and double-deck motor coaches, and motor buses."

**Traylor Engineering & Mfg. Company,
Allentown, Pennsylvania**

This Traylor mark was first used October 22, 1920, in connection with motor trucks. The company also built farm tractors and other machinery.

Triangle Motors Incorporated, Chicago, Illinois

**Truck Attachment Company,
Seattle, Washington**

No information concerning this company has surfaced, except for this mark, first used July 15, 1915.

Tucker & Sons, Grass Valley, California

SNO-CAT

This Sno-Cat mark was filed in 1944, with first use of September 1, 1941. It was for "automotive vehicles for traveling over snow."

Tucker Corporation, Chicago, Illinois

The Tucker was a sensation when introduced; this impressive trademark was first used on March 2, 1947.

Left
This mark, first used in November 1921, is for "Remanufactured Automobiles." Whether the firm actually built cars is doubtful.

Turnbull Motor Truck & Wagon Company, Defiance, Ohio

DEFIANCE

Automobiles, wagons, trucks, and other items were included in this Defiance trademark, first used November 6, 1917.

Willard Irving Twombly, New York, New York

Twombly

Twombly operated from 1913 to 1915. This mark was filed in May 1913 for "automobiles, cyclecars, and motorcycles."

U. S. Long Distance Automobile Company, Jersey City, New Jersey

LONG

DISTANCE

No information whatever has been located outside of this trademark application; it claims first use on March 27, 1900.

Union Motor Truck Company, Bay City, Michigan

"Automobiles and Automobile-Trucks" are listed as the items under this trademark. It claims first use on July 25, 1916.

Union Truck Mfg. Company Inc., New York, New York

The Union motor truck trademark shown here was first used January 1, 1916. No other information has been located.

Universal Motor Truck Company, Detroit, Michigan

Universal filed this mark in December 1912, having first used it two years previously.

Universal Motor Company, Denver, Colorado

UNIVERSAL

Automotive historians usually ascribe the year 1910 as the only one of production for the Universal. In fact, it is said to have been a promotion scheme. Yet, this mark, filed in 1912, claims first use as February 1908.

Velie Motors Corporation, Moline, Illinois

Velie began building cars in 1909 and continued for twenty years. Trucks and tractors were also built by Velie. This mark claims first use as November 16, 1902, although it was not filed until April 1919.

Victor Motors Inc., St. Louis, Missouri

1

2

Victor motor trucks first used these trademarks (1) and (2), on June 6, 1923. No other information has been located.

Viqueot Company, Long Island City, New York

VIQUEOT

The Viqueot was built during 1905 and 1906, with this mark being filed on September 21, 1905.

Vogue Motor Car Company, Tiffin, Ohio

This mark was for automobiles, automobile bodies, and motor trucks. First used June 12, 1920, the mark was filed the following month. In the automotive field, Vogue endured to 1922, but may have continued longer in making motor trucks.

**Vreeland Motor Company,
Newark, New Jersey**

No information on this company has surfaced, outside of the Ultimate mark, which was first used in July 1919.

**Walker & Barkman Mfg. Company,
Hartford, Connecticut**

The Pope-Hartford automobiles were built in the 1904-14 period, with this mark being first used about 1905.

**Walter Motor Truck Company,
Long Island City, New York**

SNOW·FIGHTER

1

First used about October 1925, no further information outside of this Snow Fighter mark (1) has been found. The 4 Point Positive Drive mark (2) for motor trucks and tractor trucks was first used December 1, 1931.

4 POINT POSITIVE DRIVE

2

**Waltham Mfg. Company,
Waltham, Massachusetts**

Auto-Go

1

Waltham built a steam carriage about 1898 and continued it for a few years. The two Auto-Go marks shown here both claim a first use of this term on September 6, 1899.

AUTOGO

2

**Ward Motor Vehicle Company,
Mt. Vernon, New York**

A rather complicated period of off-again, on-again manufacturing efforts appears for the Ward; none of them exactly mesh with the date of first use for this mark, namely, early 1911. The mark was not filed until June 1919.

Washington Motor Company, Eaton, Ohio

Operating only in the 1921-24 period, the Washington mark shown here claimed first use on May 3, 1920.

Weaver-Ebling Automobile Company, New York, New York

Historians generally indicate that manufacture was doubted for the WECO automobiles. This mark, first used in January 1915, was actually for bicycles, but again, no definite information can be located.

Weaver Manufacturing Company, Springfield, Illinois

AMBULANCE

Welch Motor Car Company, Pontiac, Michigan

Welch built cars in the 1903-11 era; this fancy script mark was filed April 1, 1909.

Westcott Motor Car Company, Springfield, Ohio

1

Beginning at Richmond, Indiana, in 1909, Westcott remained in the car business until 1925. The move to Springfield, Ohio, came in 1916. Mark (1), filed in 1917, claims first use on January 1, 1915. Mark (2) was first used February 20, 1919.

Left
The AMBULANCE mark shown here was first used in September 1913, with the description noting that it was for "vehicles for use in towing automobiles and the like."

Westcott Motor Car Company, Springfield, Ohio

2

White Motor Company, Cleveland, Ohio

1

This company began building automobiles in 1900, continuing in this endeavor until 1918. After that time the company dropped automobiles, but continued with trucks.

Mark (1) "is a facsimile of the signature of Windsor T. White, the president of the corporation." First claim to this mark is January 1909, as is mark (2) for automobiles and motor trucks. Mark (3) for White automobiles was first used in December 1913. The White Service mark (4) for "automobiles and motor trucks" went into use on July 7, 1924.

2

3

4

May 12, 1939, was the date of first use for marks (5) and (6), the famous White Horse trademarks. Mark (7) was first used January 3, 1940, and the Freightliner mark (8) came in January 1941. The White Super Power mark was first used January 3, 1937, as shown in mark (9); this mark was not filed until 1949. Three other Super Power marks, (10), (11), and (12), were first used in 1948. The modernistic design of mark (13) was first used September 26, 1958.

White Motor Company, Cleveland, Ohio

5

6

7

8

9

10

11

12

13

**Wichita Falls Motor Company,
Wichita Falls, Texas**

1

This firm built trucks from 1911 to 1932 and
produced automobiles during 1920 and 1921.
Mark (1) was first used November 15, 1911;
mark (2) saw first use January 2, 1918; and mark
(3) was adopted for use on March 17, 1925.

2

OIL FIELD SPECIAL

3

**H. E. Wilcox Motor Company,
Minneapolis, Minnesota**

WILCOX TRUX

Wilcox began by building automobiles and motor trucks, dropping the former and continuing
with the latter in 1913. This WilcoxTrux mark
was first used in 1910.

**C. H. Will Motors Corporation,
Minneapolis, Minnesota**

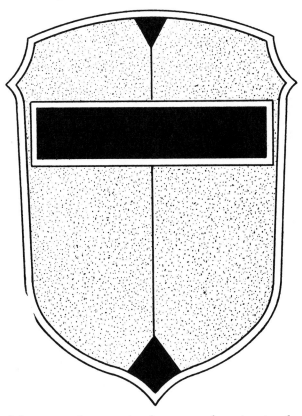

Motor coaches, motor buses, and motor trucks
were the stock-in-trade for this company. The
mark shown here was first used January 4, 1929.

Villor P. Williams, Baltimore, Maryland

The New York 6 lasted during 1927 and 1928. This interesting trademark was first used by the company on February 15, 1926, and was filed in May 1927.

Wills Sainte Claire Inc., Marysville, Michigan

1

This interesting company had an impressive trademark design. Mark (1) claimed first use on February 26, 1921, as does mark (2). However, mark (1) was filed in May 1921, whereas mark (2) was not filed until August 1926.

2

Willys-Overland Company, Toledo, Ohio

1

The history of Willys is a history unto itself. Beginning in 1909 with the Willys-Overland cars, the company went onward with many different ventures. Mark (1) of Overland is for pneumatic tires for vehicles, rather than the vehicles themselves. Mark (2) of September 1913 "is as written by John North Willys, president of the Willys Overland Company." Mark (3) for the Willys-Knight was first used November 22, 1913; another Willys-Knight mark (4) was first used November 8, 1915.

148

Willys-Overland Company, Toledo, Ohio

2

3

4

5

The Willys 6 mark (5) was first used in May 1917, and the Overland mark (6), applying to engines, was first used in June 1921. Red Bird (7), as applying to passenger cars, was first used August 1, 1923, and the Overland 6 mark (8) came into use in January 1925. The Whippet mark (9) followed in June 1926, with the Overland Whippet mark (10) coming along in January 1927. Another 1927 entry was the Collegiate trademark (11) first used in May of that year, along with the Foursome mark (12).

December 1, 1931, was the first use of mark (13), as well as mark (14). The interesting design of mark (15) was first used in November 1936.

The term "JEEP" has an interesting sidelight; this term was a trademark of King Features Syndicate with a trademark application of April 1936. In this application, mark (16), appears. It was first used March 26, 1936, "for cartoons."

6

149

RED BIRD

7

11

8

WHIPPET

9

12

OVERLAND

Whippet

10

13

14

Willys-Overland Company, Toledo, Ohio

19

15

Willys-Overland used the term "for automobiles and structural parts thereof" in mark (17), noting first use of November 20, 1940. Mark (18) was first used in February 1941, and (19) "for electric auto burglar alarms" was first used July 6, 1942.

A series of trademarks followed, indicating by their titles, some very specific applications: mark (20) for the Civijeep was first used March 15, 1945; the Agrijeep mark (21) was formalized April 15, 1944. The Jeepson mark (22) dated from June 22, 1943, and the Jeepmobile mark (23) was first used March 1, 1943. A related mark was the Civijeep. This mark (24) was first used March 15, 1945. Yet another was the Jeepster mark (25); its first use was February 11, 1943. The Jeep Buggy mark (26) was first used on March 23, 1945, and the Jeep Wagon mark (27) was first used on July 30, 1945.

JEEP

16

JEEP

17

JEEP

18

CIVIJEEP

20

AGRIJEEP

21

JEEPSON

22

JEEPMOBILE

23

CIVIJEEP

24

JEEPSTER

25

JEEP BUGGY

26

JEEP WAGON

27

PLAINSMAN

28

Willys-Overland began using the tradename Plainsman (28) for passenger carrying automobiles on January 13, 1941, and, prior to that, had begun using the Americar trademark (29) on October 15, 1940. November 5, 1946, was the date of first use for the Willys-Overland mark (30), while the Centaur mark (31) was first used October 6, 1952. The Ritz mark (32) came along with first use on March 7, 1952, and the Mechanical Mule mark (33) was first used October 8, 1953.

AMERICAR

29

Willys Overland

30

CENTAUR

31

RITZ

32

**Winfield Barnes Company,
Philadelphia, Pennsylvania**

The Adelphia mark shown here was first used June 18, 1920, apparently the only year that this car was built.

**Winther Motor Truck Company,
Kenosha, Wisconsin**

This interesting trademark design was first used for Winther motor trucks on April 2, 1917.

The Winton Company, Cleveland, Ohio

WINTON

1

Between 1896 and 1924, Winton built numerous car models. Mark (1) indicates a first use of 1892, and mark (2) for the Winton Six notes a first use of 1907.

2

Woods Mobilette Company, Chicago, Illinois

MOBILETTE

3

In the 1913-16 period, the Mobilette sought its place in the market. Mark (1) and mark (2) both indicate a first use of October 10, 1913. Trademarks (3) and (4) both go back to March 28, 1911; thus, it appears that the company was active prior to the production dates commonly assumed by automotive historians.

4

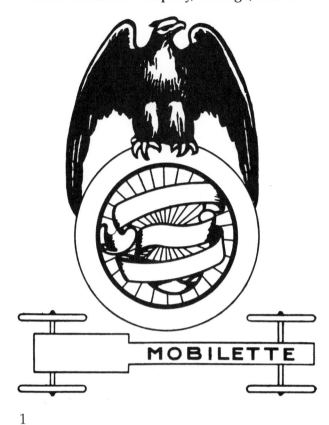

1

Wright Truck Attachment Company, Seattle, Washington

This mark, first used February 1, 1916 was for motor trucks. No other information has been located on this firm.

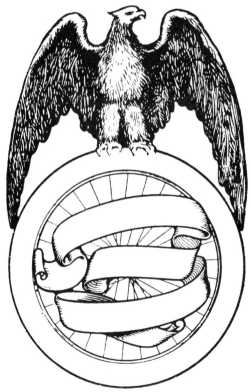

2

**Yale & Towne Mfg. Company,
Stamford, Connecticut**

YALE

The Yale automotive trucks and trailers appear to have made first use of this trademark on November 11, 1920, for motor trucks and on August 27, 1920, for trailers.

Yellow Cab Mfg. Company, Chicago, Illinois

Yellow Taxi

1

AMBASSADOR

3

Yellow Cab began at Chicago in 1915, operating there until 1928. For a couple of years after, they operated at Pontiac, Michigan.

The Yellow Taxi mark (1) was first used in July 1919. Mark (2) notes "the trademark comprises a border consisting of three rows of alternately-arranged black and white checkers. . . ." This mark was first used in June 1920. The Ambassador marks (3) and (4) were first used in December 1920.

2

AMBASSADOR

4

RedTop

5

6

7

July 25, 1922, was the date of first use for the Red Top marks (5) and (6). Yellow Cab filed the application shown at (7) on February 15, 1923. Mark (8) illustrated the color scheme used, noting that "the vertical lines in the upper part of the drawing indicate the red color of the top of the vehicles to which the trademark is applied. The vertical lines on the spinning-top emblem also denote the color red. The lower portion of the vehicle body is gray in color." This mark was first used in 1923.

The Canary mark (9) was first used in April 1923, followed by the mark shown at (10); it was first used June 20 of that year. Mark (11) was first used July 18, 1923, with mark (12) coming on July 1, 1927.

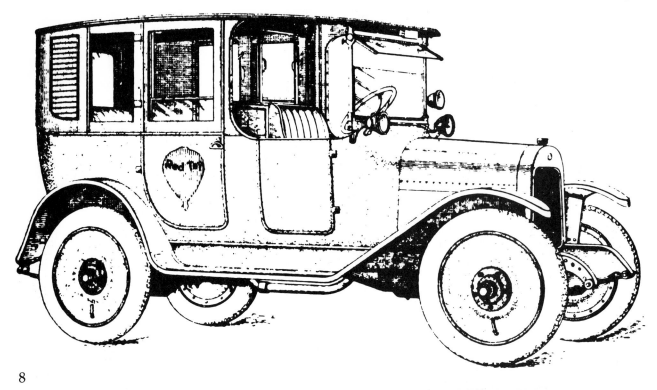

8

CANARY

9

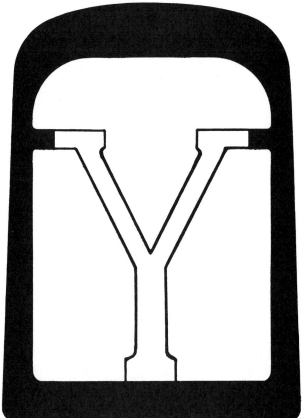

10

Yellow Cab Mfg. Company, Chicago, Illinois

11

12

Index